"Good preachers do three things with any
Jeffrey Arthurs has added one more: remind. *Preaching as Reminding* is a careful
examination of memory in the Bible, and it skillfully applies that biblical theology to the preaching craft. In a world that conveniently forgets God's truths,
this book persuades and practically points preachers back to the task of being
God's remembrancers. Seasoned and novice preachers who are serious about
their craft should heed Arthurs's call."

Desmond Soh, senior director of strategic development, associate professor of preaching,
Singapore Bible College

"*Preaching as Reminding* by Jeffrey D. Arthurs should be required reading for
every seminarian. Gordon-Conwell's professor of preaching and communication
practices what he preaches. Like a good sermon, he anchors his message that
preachers are 'remembrancers' in sound doctrine, enriched by modern science;
he then gives that truth wings to fly on the wind of know-how. Arthurs persuaded
me to be a remembrancer, freed me from the chains of novelty, and told me how
to be a good remembrancer with lightning words that strike the heart. Blessed
are those who read him, for they will be rewarded a hundredfold."

Bruce Waltke, professor emeritus of biblical studies, Regent College, Vancouver,
distinguished professor emeritus of Old Testament, Knox Theological Seminary

"Jeff Arthurs has given voice to an unspoken burden that so many preachers carry:
the drive to preach the old, old story in a new, original way. Arthurs serves as the
'remembrancer' for such preachers, reminding us that our call is not to rewrite
the Word in a unique way, but to remind congregations of the faith once delivered.
This book will serve as a blessing and a balm for all who read it."

Hope Italiano Lee, lead pastor, Kirkwood Presbyterian Church, Bradenton, Florida

"I wholeheartedly recommend this timely book to every pastor who faces the
challenge of preaching in this e-generation. With the massive amount of information on the Internet, the price of easy accessibility is the sense of priority or
focus—listening to Sunday sermons included. To preach with deeper impact,
Dr. Jeffrey Arthurs reminds us of the importance of reminding: skillfully evoking
memory in the listeners. He first expounds a theology of remembering and then
provides practical tools to stir memory in sermon preparation and delivery.
Preaching as Reminding, an excellent know-why and know-how textbook, will
definitely enrich your pulpit."

Henry Chan, senior pastor, The Rutgers Community Christian Church, Somerset, New
Jersey

"Preachers, as 'remembrancers of the Lord,' are to do what Jeffrey Arthurs beautifully and evocatively does in these pages. Offering practical guidelines, he recalls
the biblical and recent past, not just to bring it to memory, but to reactualize faith
now. In so doing, one could say he remembers the present and future as well, and
they take the shape of the gospel."

Paul Scott Wilson, professor of homiletics, Emmanuel College, University of Toronto

"With characteristic rhetorical skill and engaging style, Arthurs has gifted preachers with a biblically saturated and theologically robust vision for preaching that cultivates the church's memory. His biblical rationale is thorough, addressing the cognitive, affective, and volitional dimensions of remembrance both from a divine and human perspective, and his practical suggestions guide the preacher toward implementation. In an age of forgetfulness, I commend this book to preachers as a valuable resource that fills a modern 'homiletical hole' and challenges them to recognize and embody more fully their role as 'remembrancers.'"

Laurie Norris, associate professor of pastoral studies, Moody Bible Institute

"Drawing on biblical theology, neuroscience, and rhetorical theory, Jeffrey Arthurs makes a compelling case for preaching as the stimulation and actualization of memory. As he puts it, 'Without memory we are lost souls.' This is true of all humans, but especially of Christians who look back to God's actions and teachings in history, climaxed in the incarnation, death, and resurrection of Jesus. A must-read for pastors and would-be pastors."

Dennis P. Hollinger, president, Colman M. Mockler Distinguished Professor of Christian Ethics, Gordon-Conwell Theological Seminary

"*Preaching as Reminding* is more than just a book expounding on the riches of the art of preaching. It is, rather, a timely reminder of the responsibility of preaching in calling men and women back to the remembrance of the cross, the resurrection, and the ascension. Dr. Arthurs examines the seemingly inherent predisposition in mankind to forget and the preacher's role in awakening memory of God's covenant with man in an age that is often counterproductive to that end. Leading from a construct that all biblical preaching is a performance of reminding, Dr. Arthurs skillfully reminds us of the hope of our calling and its preeminence in a day when forgetfulness seems to be a growing trend."

Craig L. Oliver Sr., pastor, Elizabeth Baptist Church, Atlanta

"Jeffrey D. Arthurs's *Preaching as Reminding* is a remarkable contribution to the field of homiletics, ably synthesizing and integrating insights from biblical theology, neuroscience, cognitive psychology, media studies, the classical rhetorical tradition, and contemporary cultural analysis. Arthurs equips today's preachers to stir the hearts, minds, and memories of their listeners to obedient and joyful action. I heartily recommend this book to seminarians, pastors, and all those who are called to proclaim the gospel."

John Jefferson Davis, professor of systematic theology and Christian ethics, chair of the division of Christian thought, Gordon-Conwell Theological Seminary

"In *Preaching as Reminding*, Jeff Arthurs gives an in-depth study of the functions and grace of memory in the human person. In our fast-paced age that values innovation and novelty, the preacher draws us back time and again to remember the 'old, old story.' With practical advice and personal experience, Arthurs empowers today's preacher to use this great gift to draw usintimately toward God's great work among us."

Dwight Longenecker, speaker, poet, pastor, and author of *The Mystery of the Magi*

PREACHING AS REMINDING

Stirring Memory in an Age of Forgetfulness

•

JEFFREY D. ARTHURS

FOREWORD BY JOHN ORTBERG

IVP Academic

An imprint of InterVarsity Press
Downers Grove, Illinois

InterVarsity Press
P.O. Box 1400, Downers Grove, IL 60515-1426
ivpress.com
email@ivpress.com

*InterVarsity Press® is the book-publishing division of InterVarsity Christian Fellowship/USA®, a
movement of students and faculty active on campus at hundreds of universities, colleges, and schools
of nursing in the United States of America, and a member movement of the International Fellowship
of Evangelical Students. For information about local and regional activities, visit intervarsity.org.*

*Scripture quotations, unless otherwise noted, are from The Holy Bible, English Standard Version, copyright
© 2001 by Crossway Bibles, a division of Good News Publishers. Used by permission. All rights reserved.*

*While any stories in this book are true, some names and identifying information may have been changed to
protect the privacy of individuals.*

*"We Remember Jesus Christ," © 2016 Jeffrey Arthurs and Jonathan Ottoway,
used with permission.*

Cover design: Faceout Studio, Charles Brock
Interior design: Jeanna Wiggins

ISBN 978-0-8308-5190-4 (print)
ISBN 978-0-8308-8916-7 (digital)

Printed in the United States of America ∞

*InterVarsity Press is committed to ecological stewardship and to the conservation of natural resources
in all our operations. This book was printed using sustainably sourced paper.*

Library of Congress Cataloging-in-Publication Data
A catalog record for this book is available from the Library of Congress.

P	25	24	23	22	21	20	19	18	17	16	15	14	13	12	11	10	9	8	7	6	5	4	3	2	1
Y	36	35	34	33	32	31	30	29	28	27	26	25	24	23	22	21	20	19	18	17					

TO MY PASTORS, THE LORD'S REMEMBRANCERS FOR ME:

Robert Nitz, Paul Nitz, Bill Heck, Mark Coleman,

Rich Schoenert, Bobby Warrenburg

●

CONTENTS

Foreword by John Ortberg   ix

Acknowledgments   xiii

Introduction   1

1 God Remembers (and Forgets)   11

2 We Forget (and Remember)   27

3 The Lord's Remembrancers   47

4 Style as a Tool for Stirring Memory   65

5 Story as a Tool for Stirring Memory   85

6 Delivery as a Tool for Stirring Memory   103

7 Ceremony and Symbol as Tools for Stirring Memory   125

Conclusion   147

Appendix: "We Remember Jesus Christ"   149

Bibliography   151

Name and Subject Index   159

Scripture Index   163

FOREWORD

JOHN ORTBERG

●

SØREN KIERKEGAARD ONCE WROTE an essay on the difference between a genius and an apostle. A genius is a person of profound thought or extraordinary gifts—someone ahead of his or her time. An apostle is someone to whom something has happened. It is actually beside the point, he said, to note that St. Paul was a brilliant thinker or a profound stylist; Paul had been given something to point at and that was what mattered, not how well he pointed.

Apostle or genius, most of us who preach are in no danger of being mistaken for either. And yet I kept thinking of this distinction while reading through *Preaching as Reminding*.

Remembering is such a humble task. If preachers are remembrancers, as Jeffrey Arthurs says, we are the Post-it Note writers on the pages of literature and well-worn Bibles. I have had the experience of doing hours of research for a message and then trying to craft it with scholarship and imagery and awareness in a way that had never been done before, only to have the pastor giving the benediction say: "That was a good reminder."

Really?

And yet our aim as preachers is not to make people say, "Wow." It is simply to help Christ be formed in people. We do not get to choose our purpose. We do not get to choose our story.

The Scriptures themselves are the invitation to remember: Remember Abraham, Isaac, and Jacob; remember the Exodus; make a pile of stones; remember the Sabbath. Come again to the table, break the bread, drink the cup. Remember.

The problem of the human race is that we remember what we should forget ("this one thing I do; forgetting what is behind and pressing on toward what is ahead"), and we forget what we should remember. People today who have more information at their fingertips than all previous generations combined cannot remember who they are, why they are here, or what they are to do.

So it matters that we preach. It matters that we call people to remember their God and their deepest values and their truest selves and the story that has maybe shaped their lives and for sure has shaped their world. It matters that we preach with all the fidelity and urgency and learning and purity and creativity that God allows us to muster.

Ian Pitt-Watson—who shaped innumerable preachers, of whom I am one—used to say that remembering is far more than recall. When you remember something, if done right, what was present before becomes present once again. This is what we do when we come to the table, when the bread is broken and given again. In a sense it is more literal than we can imagine. Our world and the unity of the human race and our own identities have been shattered, have been dismembered. In preaching, the body of Christ is re-membered—becomes again a present, whole, and living force in the world. In preaching people can be re-minded—can have minds that are once again centered on God and therefore rooted in peace.

Preaching as Reminding wonderfully combines thoughtful wisdom about preaching with actual examples of the real thing, helping us recognize the difference between saying God is good and saying God is "still good," or the freshness of describing Christmas as a riches-to-rags story, or the assurance in the truth that however strong the storm the boat is stronger.

C. S. Lewis wrote somewhere that trying to be original is rarely productive. It's like trying to impress someone on a job interview or a first date: the attempt always inhibits the very freedom needed. But when we aim only at telling the truth—simply and thoughtfully, and in our own words—creativity has a way of coming in the side door.

Preachers are the still small voice that says, "Wake up." It does not matter how profound the message; what matters is that someone wakes up.

So read. Take notes. Learn.

Remember.

ACKNOWLEDGMENTS

•

No MAN IS AN ISLAND and no book is either. I wish to express my sincere thanks to the folks who have enriched my thinking and in many cases the text of this book. My colleagues at Gordon-Conwell Theological Seminary: Scott Gibson, Matthew Kim, Jack Davis, Tom Petter, and Gary Parrett loaned me their expertise in preaching, theology, Hebrew Bible, and worship. The board of Gordon-Conwell also granted me a generous sabbatical that allowed me to do the majority of the research and writing. Jimmie Massie gave excellent support with so many of the details of publishing, and Elissa Schauer and the editors at IVP were outstanding. My former students, now my colleagues, Alex Kato, Russell St. John, Nathan Wright, Drew Thompson, and Jared Alcántara did their part in teaching an old dog some new tricks. And my dear wife, Liz, the most delightful person I know, my dedicated proofreader, always encouraged me. I have you in my heart. Thanks be to God who has promised never to forget us, to always keep our names graven on his hands.

INTRODUCTION

There is nothing higher and stronger and more wholesome and good

for life in the future than some good memory. . . . People talk to

you a great deal about your education, but some sacred memory,

preserved from childhood, is perhaps the best education.

ALYOSHA IN *THE BROTHERS KARAMAZOV*

People need to be reminded more often than they need to be instructed.

SAMUEL JOHNSON

●

IF WE HAVE NO MEMORY we are adrift, because memory is the mooring to which we are tied. Memory of the past interprets the present and charts a course for the future.

Consider the case of Jimmie, who had Korsakoff's syndrome, a rare neurological disorder.[1] When Oliver Sacks met him in 1975, Jimmie seemed likeable, robust, and genial, not "helpless, demented, confused, and disoriented" as an outside diagnosis stated.

He walked into the doctor's office with a cheery, "Hiya, Doc! Nice morning! Do I take this chair here?" He was cooperative and answered all the questions Dr. Sacks asked. He remembered his childhood

---

[1]This fascinating nonfiction story is recounted in Oliver Sacks, *The Man Who Mistook His Wife for a Hat and Other Clinical Tales* (New York: Harper and Row, 1987), 23-42.

home, friends, and school, and he remembered joining the Navy in 1943. He had been stationed on a submarine and could still remember Morse code. He recalled, almost relived, his Navy service through the end of the war in 1945, but that's where the memories stopped. Completely stopped.

Jimmie could not remember anything from 1945 to the present (1975)—thirty years. He thought Truman was president, the periodic table stopped with uranium, and no one had been to the moon. He could not recall anything that had happened more than a few minutes in the past. He thought he was nineteen years old, not his actual forty-nine. Dr. Sacks showed him a mirror and Jimmie gazed at the middle-aged man with bushy gray hair. He was shocked!

In Dr. Sacks's words, "He suddenly turned ashen and gripped the sides of the chair. 'What's going on? What's happened to me? Is this a nightmare? Am I crazy?'"

Sacks calmed Jimmie by taking him to a window to watch a ballgame in the park below and removing the bewitching mirror. He left him alone for two minutes and then returned. Jimmie was still at the window gazing with pleasure at the kids in the park. He wheeled around with a cheery expression: "Hiya, Doc! Nice morning. You want to talk to me—do I take this chair here?" There was no sign of recognition on his frank, open face.

"Haven't we met before?" Sacks asked.

"No, I can't say we have."

Over the next nine years, Dr. Sacks and his patient were introduced and reintroduced. Jimmie stayed in the convalescent home where Sacks worked but never learned his way around the halls. He was good at rapid games of checkers and tic-tac-toe but lost at chess because the moves were too slow. Sacks had never "encountered, even imagined, such a power of amnesia, the possibility of a pit into which everything, every experience, every event would fathomlessly drop."[2] The staff at the home spoke of him as a "lost soul."

---

[2]Ibid., 35.

I'll return to Jimmie in chapter seven because there is more to the story, but this much of the narrative illustrates why I've written this book: without memory, we are lost souls. That is why the Bible is re-plete with statements, stories, sermons, and ceremonies designed to stir memory. Even nature—the rainbow after the flood—serves as a reminder of God's faithfulness (Gen 9:13-17).

The first part of this book, chapters one to three, examines biblical theology where we discover that memory is more than simple mental recall. It is re-actualization—making past things present—and it rarely divorces action and emotion from cognitive recall. In the Bible, re-membering puts together things that have been dismembered or am-putated. Chapter one shows that God remembers (and forgets), and chapter two shows that we forget (and remember). Chapter three de-scribes ministers as "the Lord's remembrancers." We remind the faithful of what they already know when knowledge has faded and conviction cooled. We fan the flames. That's what we see when we look at the work of Moses, the prophets, and the apostles.

The second section of the book takes the theology of the first three chapters and applies it to ministry to demonstrate how to stir memory through vivid language (chapter four), story (chapter five), delivery (chapter six), and ceremony (chapter seven).

The phrase "the Lord's remembrancers" was coined in 1594 by Lancelot Andrewes, chaplain to Queen Elizabeth and King James I, in a sermon titled "Remember Lot's Wife."[3] Andrewes drew his metaphor from the royal court. The king's (or queen's) remem-brancer is the oldest judicial position in continual existence in Great Britain, having been created in 1154 by Henry II. Today it is a cere-monial role, but for centuries the remembrancer's job was to put the lord treasurer and the barons of court in remembrance of pending business, taxes paid and unpaid, and other things that pertained to the benefit of the crown.

---

[3]The entire sermon can be found in Ellen F. Davis, *Imagination Shaped: Old Testament Preach-ing in the Anglican Tradition* (Valley Forge, PA: Trinity, 1995), 27-43.

Likewise, Andrewes said, preachers are the "Lord's remembrancers." We remind God's subjects of their covenant with the king of heaven. The sovereign king initiated a relationship with his people motivated by grace and sealed with his own blood, and he demands that they respond with worship, service, love, and fear.

Other cultures, especially oral cultures, also had remembrancers. The Rwandan court's specialized officials kept track of four items: lists of kings and queen mothers, important events in their reigns, the deeds and qualities of the kings, and the preservation of the secrets of the dynasty.[4] The courts of ancient Israel also had remembrancers, translated consistently in the ESV as "recorder" from the Hebrew word *zakar* ("to cause to remember") (see 2 Sam 8:15-18, 20:24; 1 Kings 4:3; 2 Kings 18:18, 37; 1 Chron 18:15; 2 Chron 34:8; Is 36:3, 22).

As part of Andrewes's exposition of Luke 17:32 where our Lord said, "Remember Lot's wife," the court preacher quotes Hebrews 2:1: "We must pay much closer attention to what we have heard, lest we drift away from it." "Drifting" is a haunting image that suggests that we can slip our mooring. The corrective, according to Andrewes, is preaching. He states that "preaching [is] employed . . . as much in calling to their minds the things they know and have forgot, as in teaching them the things they know not."[5] A century and a half later, Jonathan Edwards puts it this way: "God hath appointed . . . preaching . . . as a fit means . . . to stir up the pure minds of the saints, quicken their affections by often bringing the great things of religion to their remembrance, setting them in their proper colours, though they know them, and have been fully instructed in them."[6] One of most crucial functions preaching accomplishes, a function often neglected in homiletics textbooks, is the stirring of memory. We need not—indeed we should not—scurry about like a character in a video game searching for originality. That is not our calling.

[4]J. Vansina, *Oral Tradition* (Harmondsworth, England: Penguin, 1973), 32; cited in Alan Baddeley, *Your Memory: A User's Guide* (New York: Macmillan, 2004), 202.
[5]Davis, *Imagination Shaped*, 30. See also Lisa Washington Lamb, *Blessed and Beautiful: Multiethnic Churches and the Preaching that Sustains Them* (Eugene, OR: Cascade, 2014), 181.
[6]Jonathan Edwards, "Treatise Concerning the Religious Affections," *The Works of Jonathan Edwards*, ed. John E. Smith (New Haven, CT: Yale University Press, 1959), 2:115-16.

Both Andrewes and Edwards were probably aware of Augustine's profound meditations on memory in the *Confessions* in which he suggests why memory must be stirred. Using the metaphor of the cave, he describes how we shove things we have learned into hidden recesses so that unless they are drawn out by admonition, we will never think of them.[7] Augustine also compares memory to a storehouse and field.[8] A remembrancer is a servant who brings things from the storehouse, a farmer who helps the listener harvest memories previously planted.[9] Augustine's most striking metaphor for memory may be the "stomach of the mind" (*venter animi*) where food is stored without tasting but later brought forth for rumination.[10] This metaphor strikes the modern ear as odd and even repulsive, but the image is brilliant. It implies that memories are held and digested, eventually nourishing the whole body. The remembrancer helps people ruminate.

Today's metaphors for memory have moved away from storage to mechanisms of capturing and sorting. In the twentieth century the camera metaphor was popular, conceiving of memory as catching images on blank film. Today we favor the computer metaphor to suggest how our minds sort and retrieve data.[11] Both of these have merit, but as with all metaphors they obscure as well as reveal. They imply that memories are always accurate because they are captured and stored mechanically, but, as we will see in chapter two, this is not the case. Humans are not machines. For one thing, we forget; and for another, we actively select, highlight, and discard elements from the past to form a cohesive narrative that makes sense in the present.

To counter the human propensity to edit memories, God has given us narrative and ceremony. The majority of the Bible is narrative,

---

[7] Augustine, *Confessions*, 10.10.17.

[8] Ibid., 10.8.12.

[9] Lamb, *Blessed and Beautiful*, 139. To see this in practice, consult the most enchanting passage on memory I am aware of in English literature—the first chapter of *David Copperfield*, where the narrator reaches as far back as memory allows into early childhood. As Augustine might say, he reaches deep into the cave or storehouse to bring forth dusty objects into the light of day. Read it with delight.

[10] Augustine, *Confessions*, 10.14.21-22.

[11] Lamb, *Blessed and Beautiful*, 100.

a fixed account of God's action in redemptive history, and he commands children of the covenants to recall those actions with concrete ceremonies such as the Passover and the Lord's Supper.

However we describe it—using images of cave, storehouse, field, stomach, camera, or computer—one of the preacher's main callings is to make knowledge, values, and experience present once again. Ministers must serve as the Lord's remembrancers because things learned can be buried, lost, amputated, or corrupted. That is why Peter said, "I intend always to remind you of these qualities, though you know them. . . . I think it right, as long as I am in this body, to stir you up by way of reminder" (2 Pet 1:12-13). Ministers take their cue from Peter, devoting themselves to the work of stirring memory. Chapter two returns to this issue, arguing that the ministry of reminding was central, not peripheral, in the preaching of Moses in Deuteronomy, in the work of God's spokespeople in the Prophets, and in the teaching of the apostles in the Epistles.

A word of caution is needed here: nagging dwells next door to reminding. No one likes to be nagged. The incessant twang of a one-string banjo quickly annoys. Nagging implies superior authority, knowledge, and morality. It is nettlesome and meddlesome, but "reminding" and "repeating" are not synonyms. Ministers must learn to *stir* memory, not simply repeat threadbare platitudes. We must rouse that which is already present within the child of God: knowledge of our Father's love and majesty.

I hope preaching as reminding strikes you as good news if you have been shamed into believing that every sermon has to include novel ideas. No. Telling the old, old story stands in the front rank of the preacher's calling. Some may raise a skeptical eyebrow. "Preaching as reminding sounds monotonous," they say. "Repeating what believers have heard since they were children sounds like a homiletical nightmare, like preaching Christmas fifty-two weeks a year." But when it is done well, preaching as reminding is not empty repetition, formalistic and perfunctory. Rather, it is the work of soul-watchers. Our people need reminders of the great truths of the faith. We are like the hobbits who "liked to have books filled with things that they already knew, set out fair and square with no contradictions."[12] Not only do people need reminders, but they also enjoy them.

WHAT REMINDING DOES

Stirring memory does many things for our listeners.

Prompts thankfulness. As we model how to count our blessings, naming them one by one, others will be moved to gratitude. "Oh give thanks to the LORD. . . . Remember the wondrous works that he has done, his miracles, and the judgments he uttered" (Ps 105:1, 5).

Raises hope. As we pull from the storehouse stories of God's work in the past, we stir hope. That's what the psalmist did when he suffered: "Will the LORD spurn forever, and never again be favorable? . . . I will remember the deeds of the LORD; yes, I will remember your wonders of old" (Ps 77:7, 11).

Prompts repentance. We cannot mourn what we have forgotten, so preaching as reminding helps people repent. The story of Peter's denials illustrates the relationship of memory to repentance: "Peter remembered the saying of Jesus, 'Before the rooster crows, you will deny me three times.' And he went out and wept bitterly" (Mt 26:75).

Fosters humility. Humility walks hand in hand with memory. During the festival of First Fruits, the Israelites were to recite, "A wandering Aramean was my father" (Deut 26:5). They were to remind themselves of their history as nomads and outcasts and that God had brought them to the land flowing with milk and honey.

Helps believers walk wisely. As we remind listeners of what they already know, we help them walk wisely in the fear of the Lord. One of the chief ends of learning is the organization of disjointed memories into coherent understanding. The present can be appreciated only when viewed in light of what has come before, just as an individual note of music makes sense only in the context of other notes.

---

[12]J. R. R. Tolkien, *The Fellowship of the Ring* (New York: Ballantine Books, 1954), 9.

Warns of unbelief and disobedience. That is how Jesus (and Lancelot Andrewes) uses the memory of Lot's wife (Lk 17:32). By reminding listeners of a woman who disobeyed, Jesus warns the listeners that they should not do so. Lancelot Andrewes says some stories urge us to *memento et fuge*—"remember and flee."[13]

Encourages belief and obedience. As we recount stories in Scripture, we hold up not just examples for warning but also examples for emulation. Andrewes describes this as *memento et fac*—"remember and do likewise." The story of the woman at Bethany who anointed Jesus with very expensive nard has been told and retold around the world (Mk 14:9), stirring other disciples to follow her example of extravagant worship.

Prompts mercy. As we remind the covenant community that they have received mercy, they will be moved to show mercy. That is the spiritual motivation of Deuteronomy 24:17-18: "You shall not pervert the justice due to the sojourner or to the fatherless, or take a widow's garment in pledge, but you shall remember that you were a slave in Egypt." Israel was to remember that they were oppressed in Egypt, so they should not be oppressors themselves.

Forms individual and communal identity. Just as the Jews lived as exiles in Babylon, so New Testament believers live as aliens and exiles in this world, and the world can squeeze them into its mold. The present reality can seem to be the only reality, so preachers remind the exiles, "Do not forget who you are and whose you are. Do not forget where you came from and where you are going." The remembrancer named Jeremiah puts it this way: "Remember the LORD from far away, and let Jerusalem come into your mind" (Jer 51:50). Old Testament scholar Walter Brueggemann observes that when "we have completely forgotten our past, we will absolutize the present and we will be like contented cows in Bashan who want nothing more than the best of today. . . . It takes a powerful articulation of memory to maintain a sense of identity in the midst of exile."[14] Preaching as reminding provides that articulation.

---

[13]Lamb, *Blessed and Beautiful*, 194.
[14]Walter Brueggemann, *Hopeful Imagination: Prophetic Voices in Exile* (Philadelphia: Fortress, 1986), 102.

To guard against our tendency to drift, Jesus gave the Holy Spirit, the Helper, to bring to mind all that he had said (Jn 14:26). As this book argues, one of the primary agencies of the Holy Spirit is the ministry of pastors who anchor believers to "the faith that was once for all delivered to the saints" (Jude 3). So we take up our task in buoyancy and hope—the task of sharpening our skills in stirring memory—because the Lord God has commissioned and equipped ministers to serve as the Lord's remembrancers.

1

GOD REMEMBERS
(AND FORGETS)

Jesus, remember me when you come into your kingdom.

LUKE 23:42

Can a woman forget her nursing child,

that she should have no compassion on the son of her womb?

Even these may forget, yet I will not forget you.

Behold, I have engraved you on the palms of my hands.

ISAIAH 49:15-16

●

MEMORY IS ONE OF THE principle themes of *The Silver Chair*, the fourth book in C. S. Lewis's Narnia series.[1] In it Lewis tells the tale of Jill and Eustace who undertake a mission from Aslan to free Prince Rilian, who is held captive by the evil queen of Underland, a subterranean world of caves and shadows. The queen has Rilian under a spell so that he does not remember Overworld, the land of Narnia, the sun, or Aslan himself. But every night Rilian has a moment of lucidity when the spell fades and memories flash. During those moments—his

---

[1]C. S. Lewis, *The Silver Chair* (New York: Macmillan, 1953). This portion of the story is found on pages 151-59.

only moments of true sanity—the queen binds him to the silver chair so that his memories torment him but he cannot act on them.

One night the brave trio of Jill, Eustace, and Puddleglum the Marsh-wiggle manage to free the prince from the chair before the spell takes hold again. Rilian sees clearly and longs to return to Overworld to feel again the bracing air of Narnia, but the queen has more tricks up her sleeve. She befuddles the four subjects of Aslan by throwing green powder on a fire, producing "a sweet and drowsy smell." Thrumming hypnotically on a mandolin, she coos, "Narnia? Narnia? I have often heard your Lordship utter that name in your ravings. Dear Prince, you are very sick. There is no land called Narnia."

Puddleglum and the others gamely argue with her: they have been in Narnia! They have seen it! She counters, "Tell me, I pray you, where that country is?" The only response the muddled Marsh-wiggle can offer is, "Up there, I don't know exactly where."

"Is there a country up among the stones and mortar of the roof?" the queen purrs.

"I've seen the sky full of stars," the stout Marsh-wiggle contends. "I've seen the sun coming up out of the sea of a morning and sinking behind the mountains at night. And I've seen him up in the midday sky when I couldn't look at him for brightness."

This rouses the others. How could they have forgotten? Of course! They had all seen the sun.

The queen feels the tide of the argument turning against her but explains that the "sun" is merely a projection of Underworld's "lamp": "Your sun is a dream, and there is nothing in that dream that was not copied from the lamp."

She says the same of Aslan. The so-called lion is like a huge cat, nothing more. Thrumming her instrument, she states, "You can put nothing into your make-believe without copying it from the real world, this world of mine, which is the only world."

The queen has regained the upper hand and is about to declare victory, but suddenly, gathering all his strength, Puddleglum stamps out the fire and rouses his memories. They are so strong that even if those things were made up—trees, grass, sun, moon, stars, and Aslan himself—then the "made-up things seem a good deal more important than the real ones."

"I'm going to live as like a Narnian as I can even if there isn't any Narnia," he declares.

The children and the prince snap out of the spell—"Hurrah! Good old Puddleglum!"—and overthrow the queen.

That's what memory can do. It makes the past present and charts a course for the future.

MEMORY IN THE BIBLE

In the Bible, "remembering" is more than mental recall. It involves emotion and volition as well as cognition.[2] It not only touches the past; it also articulates with the present and the future, helping a person connect previously acquired wisdom to current and future decisions. In the words of Old Testament scholar Robert Cosand, "Remembrance is an understanding of the reality of the past in such a way that the events of the past become a force in the present, producing some activity of will or of body or both."[3] Bruce Waltke says simply, "Remembrance equals participation."[4] When God remembers, he blesses. His mind, emotions, and actions favor the object of his attention. Or phrased in a more Hebraic way, his face is toward us, his eye is on us, and his hand is with us.

That's what we hear when the thief on the cross asks the Lord to remember him (Lk 23:42). He means, of course, "Please extend your grace to me in the hour of death and especially in the hour following death." We've lost much of this rich connotation of the word "remember" in modern English, but even today we hear an echo of the

---

[2]Edward P. Blair, "An Appeal to Remembrance: The Memory Motif in Deuteronomy," *Interpretation* 15 (1961): 43.

[3]J. Robert Cosand, "The Theology of Remembrance in the Cultus of Israel" (PhD diss., Trinity Evangelical Divinity School, 1995), 293.

[4]Bruce Waltke, *An Old Testament Theology* (Grand Rapids: Zondervan, 2007), 504. Waltke is quoting Brevard S. Childs, who has written a thorough study of memory in *Memory and Tradition in Israel*, Studies in Biblical Theology 37 (Naperville, IL: Allenson, 1962).

biblical emphasis when the child at the party sees the host passing out treats. Bobbing in her seat and waving her hand, she pleads, "Remember me!" Look on me with favor. Similarly, we say, "The company always remembers its employees at Christmas."

Not only does memory in the Bible equal participation and blessing, it also "re-members" disconnected things. At times this life seems inchoate, a tale told by an idiot signifying nothing, but reminders of God's power in the past, his presence in the present, and his promises for the future help God's children believe in the unseen hand that guides the affairs of their lives. Memory reunites us mentally, emotionally, and volitionally to the God who watches over us.

Even though our modern concept of memory is thinner than the biblical concept, our ceremonies and monuments maintain the robust sense. Perhaps you've been to the Vietnam Veterans Memorial in Washington, DC, descending along its two walls sunk into the ground. As of May 2014, 58,300 names were etched into the reflective black rock. Perhaps you have found the experience, as I have, to be somber and sobering. Cognitive recall of the past is brought into the present so that the visitor participates vicariously in the tragedy of the war.

If you visit Kings Domain Park in Melbourne, Australia, you may have a similar experience at the Shrine of Remembrance. It commemorates soldiers from the state of Victoria who died in World War I. Paving stones outside the shrine state, "We will remember them," and one of the interior walls bears this exhortation: "Let all men know that this is holy ground. This shrine, established in the hearts of men as on the solid earth, commemorates a people's fortitude and sacrifice. Ye therefore that come after, give remembrance." In the center of the shrine is the Stone of Remembrance on which is inscribed, "Greater love hath no man," and on November 11 at 11 a.m. (Remembrance Day), the sun shines through a small aperture in the roof to illumine the word "love."

Is it worth the time and expense to build and maintain those memorials and the thousands of others like them around the world? We believe it is. The Pearl Harbor Memorial in Honolulu, the Tomb of the Unknown Soldier in Arlington, Virginia, the Kigali Genocide Memorial, and the site of the Pilgrims' first Thanksgiving at Plimoth Plantation, Massachusetts, give testimony to our conviction that the past should not be allowed to fade from consciousness. To ensure that this does not happen we need reminders.

Perhaps the most sobering of all memorials in the United States is the Holocaust Museum in Washington, DC. When you enter you are given a "passport" that presents brief biographical facts about an actual Holocaust victim, and you then walk through the museum, which is laid out chronologically, noting what happened to your character each year. The museum is intended to help visitors remember the past through more than simple cognition. It creates a vicarious experience. When I visited the museum I received the passport of a cobbler in Warsaw in 1936. I first experienced the cobbler's joys of family and community, but then in 1939 the story turned dark as we were walled into the ghetto. Eventually the story reached its nadir when we were sent to Buchenwald in the early forties. Nothing is known about the cobbler after that.

Why build such a museum? Is it to lament the past? Yes. Is it to make the abstract concrete? Yes. But the primary purpose is to keep memory alive, honoring the dead and warning the living. After the Battle of Gettysburg, Abraham Lincoln dedicated another memorial with these words: "We here highly resolve that these dead shall not have died in vain—that this nation, under God, shall have a new birth of freedom—and that government of the people, by the people, and for the people, shall not perish from the earth." Memorials cause us to look back but also to look forward.

BIBLICAL TERMS FOR "REMEMBER"

In the Old Testament the Hebrew word *zakar* is the primary term for "remember." It is used more than two hundred times in various forms and, as we have seen, rarely means simple mental recall. The same is true of the *mimnēskō* word group in the New Testament. It is used seventy-four times, appearing in every book except 1 Timothy, 1 Peter, and 1 and 2 John. Both *zakar* and *mimnēsko* demonstrate that memory is a whole-person activity. Using Brevard Childs's term, biblical memory is "actualization."[5]

MEMORY IN THE BIBLE IS A WHOLE-PERSON ACTIVITY

The following verses indicate that in the Bible memory is more than cognitive recall. It is a whole-person activity that includes the mind, emotions, and will.

Exodus 20:8. "Remember the Sabbath day, to keep it holy." This means, of course, that Israel was to sanctify the Sabbath by taking action—worshiping and resting.

Genesis 40–41. While in jail, Joseph blesses the cupbearer by interpreting his dream. He asks the cupbearer to remember him before Pharaoh once he is freed, but the "chief cupbearer did not remember Joseph, but forgot him" (Gen 40:23). Later the cupbearer realizes his mistake and speaks favorably of Joseph to Pharaoh (Gen 41:9).

Deuteronomy 15:15. Israel is to remember the days of their slavery in Egypt as a motive for freeing their own slaves every six years.

Joshua 1:13, 16-17. As the nation of Israel stands at the Jordan, poised to enter the Promised Land, Joshua urges them, "Remember the word that Moses the servant of the LORD commanded you, saying, 'The LORD your God is providing you a place of rest and will give you this land.' . . . And they answered Joshua, 'All that you have commanded us we will do, and wherever you send us we will go. Just as we obeyed Moses in all things, so we will obey you.'"

Galatians 2:10. "Remember the poor."

Colossians 4:18. "Remember my chains."

---

[5]Childs, *Memory and Tradition*, 82. Similarly, Robert Cosand states, "Remembrance produces activity. If one remembers one's sin, then shame and repentance are the results. If one remembers God, then praise or obedience results. When God remembers sin, He punishes it. When He remembers a person, His grace is bestowed on that person. When He remembers His covenant with Abraham, He acts in accordance with what He promised and grants His favor to Israel." Cosand, "Theology of Remembrance," 112.

Hebrews 13:3. "Remember those who are in prison."

Hebrews 13:7. "Remember your leaders, those who spoke to you the word of God. Consider the outcome of their way of life, and imitate their faith."

Revelation 2:5. "Remember therefore from where you have fallen; repent, and do the works you did at first."

Revelation 3:3. "Remember, then, what you received and heard. Keep it, and repent."

The character of *zakar* can be seen by the company it keeps, the synonyms that nuance it. Some of the synonyms used regularly are "keep" (or "guard"), "listen" (or "obey"), and "show favor." Psalm 103:17-18 states that the Lord's steadfast love is upon "those who fear him . . . to those who keep his covenant and remember to do his commandments." Likewise, the festival of Purim "should be remembered and kept throughout every generation" (Esther 9:28).

Four synonyms cluster in one passage, Exodus 2:24-25: "God *heard* their groaning, and God *remembered* his covenant with Abraham, with Isaac, and with Jacob. God *saw* the people of Israel—and God *knew.*"[6] Theologically we understand that God's memory cannot be jarred; rather, the author of Exodus uses the cluster of synonyms to speak of God's faithfulness, omniscience, and tender regard for the enslaved children of Israel. The terms beautifully depict divine cognition, emotion, and volition—God's "whole person" response—on behalf of his people. That was the encouragement the original readers of Exodus needed, a reminder that God is faithful to his covenant.

The disciples would need similar encouragement after Jesus departed this earth. Jesus implies that they would feel abandoned like orphans (Jn 14:18), so he comforts them with these words: "The Holy Spirit, whom the Father will send in my name, he will . . . bring to your remembrance all that I have said to you. Peace I leave with you" (Jn 14:26-27). The Spirit's ministry of remembrance brings peace as it assures troubled hearts that God has not forsaken them.

---

[6]Emphasis added.

The opposite of remembering, of course, is forgetting, and this term also implies more than lack of mental recall. Forgetting is parallel to "forsaking" and "rejecting." Isaiah 49:14 states, "The Lord has forsaken me; my Lord has forgotten me." Similarly, Hosea 4:6-7 states, "Because you have rejected knowledge, . . . And since you have forgotten the law of your God, I will also forget your children."

To forget God means to disobey the commandments and worship other gods: "Take care lest you forget the Lord your God by not keeping his commandments. . . . If you forget the Lord your God and go after other gods and serve them and worship them . . . you shall surely perish" (Deut 8:11, 19). Judges 3:7 shows that the warning of Deuteronomy came true: "The people of Israel did what was evil in the sight of the Lord. They forgot the Lord their God and served the Baals and the Asheroth."

Conversely, the one who does not forget God fears him, delights in his statutes and does not stray from his precepts:

> I will delight in your statutes;
> I will not forget your word. (Ps 119:16)

> I do not forget your law. . . .
> I do not stray from your precepts. (Psalm 119:109-110)

In the Bible, emotion and volition link arms with cognition as memory brings the past into the present with compelling power, producing appropriate behavior.

GOD REMEMBERS

"What is man that you are mindful of him?" (Ps 8:4). The word for "mindful" in this verse is the same term we have been exploring—*zakar*. Here, to be mindful is to remember. The psalmist asks this because even though humans are crowned with glory and honor, we are also as insubstantial as a wind that passes (Ps 78:39), mist that vanishes (Jas 4:14), and grass that withers (Ps 90:5-6). God remembers that we are only dust (Ps 103:14) and we would do well to remember also.

The Trappist monks certainly do. Known for their austere lifestyle, these brothers have a specific discipline regarding burial. When one of the monks dies, the rest of the order places his body in a newly dug grave, and immediately after the interment they trace the dimensions of a new grave, the resting place of the next brother who will die, whoever he may be. In this way they remind themselves of their own mortality and thus gain wisdom for living.

Psalm 56 contains a poignant image of how God remembers our low estate. When David was being pursued by the Philistines, he lamented that "man tramples on me" (Ps 56:1), "all their thoughts are against me for evil" (Ps 56:5), and "they lurk; they watch my steps," waiting for a chance to capture him (Ps 56:6). The anxiety and stress kept David awake at night and provoked many tears, and in all those fitful, wakeful hours, God was present:

> You have kept count of my tossings;
>> put my tears in your bottle.
> Are they not in your book? (Ps 56:8)

In the ancient world people sometimes collected and kept their tears in a small bottle as a memorial of their grief. God so identifies with his people that he puts our tears into his bottle and writes them in his book. When the Heavenly Father remembers, he answers prayer (Gen 30:22), blesses (Ps 115:12-13), saves us from our enemies (Num 10:9), protects (Gen 19:29), and rescues (Ps 136:23-24).

God's tender regard for his children arises in part because of the incarnation. Made in the likeness of men, God tabernacled among us, and as the King James Version says, he is "touched with the feeling of our infirmities" (Heb 4:15). Not only did he condescend to become human, he also lowered himself by taking the form of a servant. Born in a stable, growing up with the indignities of poverty and oppression, maligned for doing good, and dying the death of a slave, Jesus knows our troubles.

God remembers all people, as he declared to Noah with the sign of the rainbow (Gen 8:1; 9:15-16), but he particularly remembers the subjects of the covenant. When God solemnly obligates himself with a vow, he never forgets. In a world of spin and hype, the Christian rests on the assurance that God's yes is yes and his no is no. He is true to his word spoken to Abraham and his descendants: "I will remember my covenant with Jacob, and I will remember my covenant with Isaac and my covenant with Abraham, and I will remember the land" (Lev 26:42). The promise made to Abraham still stands: "I will bless you and make your name great, so that you will be a blessing. . . . In you all the families of the earth shall be blessed" (Gen 12:2-3).

That promise has been fulfilled in Jesus Christ, the offspring of Abraham, so that now all who believe in Christ are the spiritual offspring of the patriarch. Zechariah articulates that confidence at the birth of his son, John the Baptist: he does not forget "to show the mercy promised to our fathers and to remember his holy covenant, the oath that he swore to our father Abraham" (Lk 1:72-73).

God has blessed all the families of the world by sending his Son—his only Son, the Son whom he loves—as the sacrifice for sins. On the night he was betrayed, Jesus instituted a new covenant with his own blood, the fulfillment of the old covenant that had been ratified with the blood of circumcision and animal sacrifices. The blood of bulls and goats could never take away sins, but when Jesus offered his own body as a single sacrifice for the sins of humanity, once for all, he sat down at the right hand of God, and now he remembers our sins and lawless deeds no more (Heb 10:11-17).

God's remembrance is one of the towering peaks in the theological Himalayas, which also include his grace, majesty, and power. Doxology is the appropriate response, lifting our hands and voices in response to his promise "I will never leave you nor forsake you" (Heb 13:5). The Greek text of this verse contains five negative particles, cumbersome to render into English, but soul-enriching nevertheless: "Never will I leave you—no, never—no! Nor forsake you." The hymn "How Firm a Foundation" recreates that purposeful redundancy:

> The soul that on Jesus hath leaned for repose
> I will not, I will not desert to its foes;

That soul, though all hell should endeavor to shake,
I'll never, no never, no never forsake![7]

An old hymn by James Montgomery is sometimes sung on Maundy Thursday. Through five stanzas it exhorts worshipers to remember God—"I will remember Thee," "I must remember Thee," and so forth. But the last verse provides a reality check, for no matter how well we remember God, we falter. Thus, the hymn concludes:

And when these failing lips grow dumb
And mind and memory flee,
When Thou shalt in Thy kingdom come,
Jesus, remember me.[8]

The believer's hope rests in the Savior's memory.

When we are reminded of God's remembrance, we respond in doxology, but we also take warning because at times God's recollection means judgment. This is true in a general sense when God's wrath is poured out on all sinners (Rom 1:18, 28; 2:1-5), and it is true in a specific sense with the symbolic city of Babylon in the book of Revelation: "God remembered Babylon the great, to make her drain the cup of the wine of the fury of his wrath" because "her sins are heaped high as heaven, and God has remembered her iniquities" (Rev 16:19; 18:5).

While sinners outside of the covenant rightly quake lest they fall into the hands of an angry God, his judgment on children in the covenant should be thought of as discipline, not retribution. Punishment is for training so that God's people will trust and obey, the only way to be happy in the Lord. As the author of Hebrews states, quoting Proverbs 3,

My son, do not regard lightly the discipline of the Lord,
    nor be weary when reproved by him.
The Lord disciplines the one he loves,
    and chastises every son whom he receives. (Heb 12:5-6)

---

[7]Author unknown, "How Firm a Foundation," 1787. Commonly attributed to Robert Keene.
[8]James Montgomery, "According to Thy Gracious Word," 1825.

This may be a subtle difference—hating the sin but loving the sinner—but it is a subtlety that gives heart. God does not condemn his subjects who slip in their obedience. Rather, he condemns their sin by nailing it to the cross, and then he trains disciples in right living.

God disciplines his children because a covenant is a solemn agreement between a sovereign and his people. The king agrees to provide for the citizens and they agree to obey his laws. The king of heaven initiated the covenant unilaterally, sovereignly, and graciously, and once the covenant is sealed with blood and vows, the subjects must fulfill their duties. One of the minister's primary responsibilities is reminding the faith family of God's grace extended in Jesus—the new covenant—and our fitting response of obedience. Like the king's remembrancer who put the barons in mind of their duties to the crown, the Lord's remembrancers remind the covenant people of their duty to love God and neighbor.

WE ASK GOD TO REMEMBER

Because God is true to his word, it is perfectly natural for his children to cry out when they suffer, "Remember me!" and "Remember us!" When humiliated before the Philistines, Samson prays, "O Lord GOD, please remember me and please strengthen me only this once, O God, that I may be avenged on the Philistines" (Judg 16:28). When pleading for mercy, Job asks God to "remember that my life is a breath" (Job 7:7). Similarly, the author of Lamentations surveys his besieged city and cries out, "Remember, O LORD, what has befallen us; look, and see our disgrace!" (Lam 5:1).

The greatest repository in the Bible for this kind of prayer is the psalms of lament, especially the imprecatory psalms. For example, Ethan, the author of Psalm 89, prays, "Remember, O Lord, how your servants are mocked" (Ps 89:50). Similarly, Asaph beseeches God, "Arise, O God, defend your cause; remember how the foolish scoff at you all the day!" (Ps 74:22). Over and over the poets ask God to remember his suffering people.

"Remember me; remember us!" achieves its shrillest pitch in the imprecatory psalms, but that same prayer is also naturally breathed out in supplication. Perhaps you recall Lancelot Andrewes from the introduction of this book, the man who coined the phrase "the Lord's remembrancers." Andrewes was a brilliant scholar, supervising much of the translation of the King James Version of the Bible, and he was also a deeply devout man. We can learn much from the prayers he used for his private devotions. Each set of daily prayers is permeated with Scripture. The following passage is a portion of his intercession for the fourth day, in which, like the psalmists, he asks God to remember . . . remember . . . remember:

> Remember to crown the year with Thy goodness; for the eyes of all wait upon Thee, and Thou givest them their meat in due season.
>
> Remember Thy holy Church, from one end of the earth to the other; and establish her unto the end of the world.
>
> Remember every Christian soul in affliction, distress, and trial,
>
> Moreover, Lord, remember graciously our holy fathers, the honourable presbytery, and all the clergy, rightly dividing the word of truth
>
> Those who are on trial, in mines, in exile, in galleys, in whatever affliction, necessity, and emergency, remember, O God.
>
> Those of whom we have not made mention, through ignorance, forgetfulness, or number of names, do Thou Thyself remember, O God, Thou who knowest each man and his petition, each house, and its need.[9]

A theology of memory shows us that the God of the covenant is true to his word and to his children, so we are bold, like Lancelot Andrewes, to ask him to remember us.

GOD FORGETS

Like remembering, forgetting is a whole-person activity of mind, will, and emotion. For ancient believers, being remembered by God, family, and community was tantamount to possessing honor and identity. Thus Nehemiah prayed, "Remember for my good, O my God, all that

---

[9]Lancelot Andrewes, *Lancelot Andrewes and His Private Devotions*, trans. Alexander Whyte (Grand Rapids: Baker, 1981), 99-103.

I have done for this people" (Neh 5:19), and "Remember me, O my
God, concerning this, and do not wipe out my good deeds that I have
done for the house of my God" (Neh 13:14; see also Neh 13:22, 31).
Conversely, God's forgetting means he judges. Our salvation, hope,
identity, and even our very existence are possible only because God
remembers us, so when he forgets, life sputters and ceases.

One way the Bible refers to being remembered is to say a person's
"name" lives on because one's "name" is a shorthand way to denote the
whole of a person's essence. Absalom worried that he would be forgotten
because he had "no son to keep [his] name in remembrance," so he built
a pillar and modestly named it "Absalom's monument" (2 Sam 18:18).
Conversely, the Lord assures eunuchs in the covenant that God will give
them "a monument and a name better than sons and daughters; I will
give them an everlasting name that shall not be cut off" (Is 56:5).

Therefore, because existence and honor are linked to being remembered, the possibility that one's name might be forgotten appears in Scripture as a severe menace. The phrases "May his name
not be remembered" and "May his memory be blotted out" were
ways to curse an enemy (see Job 18:17; Ps 9:5-6; 83:4; 109:14; Prov
10:7; Jer 11:19). The failure to be remembered is a dire punishment
from God, synonymous with obliteration (see Ex 17:14; Deut 32:26;
Is 26:14; Eccles 9:5).

God does not forget his children, but he does forget their sins:
"Though your sins are like scarlet, they shall be as white as snow" (Is
1:18). Of course, on one level it is impossible for God to forget anything. But in keeping with what we have seen about remembering and
forgetting, we understand that when the Bible says he forgets our sins,
it means he does not act toward us on the basis of those sins. They no
longer bear on our relationship. In Edward Blair's words, "To forget
something . . . is to let the past fall out of dynamic, conditioning relation to the present."[10] The story of Shimei and David is an analogy
of God's forgetting our sins: when Shimei begs King David not to

---

[10]Blair, "Appeal to Remembrance," 44.

remember his insults (2 Sam. 19:19), he does not expect the king to mentally jettison them but rather to volitionally jettison them—that is, to not act toward Shimei in accord with the disloyal deed.

Because God forgets our sins, we should too, not with cavalier forgetfulness that fails to recognize the pit from which we were drawn but with buoyant forgetfulness that is no longer haunted by past rebellion or future retribution. Such buoyancy is possible because our hope is in Christ: "Remember Jesus Christ. . . . If we have died with him, we will also live with him" (2 Tim 2:8-11).

Alluding to Isaiah 49:16 ("Behold, I have engraved you on the palms of my hands"), Charles Wesley wrote:

> Arise, my soul, arise; shake off thy guilty fears;
> The bleeding sacrifice in my behalf appears:
> Before the throne my surety stands,
> My name is written on His hands.[11]

As practical theology, preaching as reminding is built on theology proper—the character and actions of God. Because he remembers his covenant and forgets the sins of his children, promising never to leave or forsake them, ministers take their stance as the Lord's remembrancers, reminding the baptized that nothing shall separate them from the love of God in Christ Jesus. But preaching as reminding is built on a second foundation also, one related to human nature: we are prone to forget.

---

[11]Charles Wesley, "Arise, My Soul, Arise," 1742.

2

WE FORGET
(AND REMEMBER)

Education is what survives when what has been learnt has been forgotten.

B. F. SKINNER

We write our benefits in dust and our injuries in marble. . . .
It ought not so to be. If our memories
were more tenacious of the merciful visitations of our God
our faith would often be strengthened in times of trial.

CHARLES HADDON SPURGEON

Lord God of Hosts, be with us yet,
Lest we forget—lest we forget.

KIPLING, "RECESSIONAL"

●

You WILL REMEMBER Jill and Eustace as the main characters of C. S. Lewis's *The Silver Chair*.[1] Early in the story, these two escape from school bullies by taking a magic door through a wall to discover that they are "out of the school grounds, out of England, out of our whole world into That Place." While walking through "That Place"

---

[1]This portion of the story is taken from C. S. Lewis, *The Silver Chair* (New York: Macmillan, 1953), 8-21.

(is it heaven?) in an open wood they come suddenly to the edge of a cliff so high that they look down on enormous white clouds that look no bigger than fluffy sheep far below.

On that towering cliff Aslan appears to Jill and Eustace and commissions them to find the lost prince in Narnia, the land far below: "Seek this lost Prince until either you have found him and brought him to his father's house, or else died in the attempt, or else gone back into your own world."

But how will they find him? No one has seen the prince for years! No one knows where he is! Aslan gives Jill four signs to guide her— specific sights and occurrences that will happen along the way— and he insists that she memorize the signs by repeating them again and again until she can say them perfectly. Then Aslan issues this solemn warning:

> Remember, remember, remember the Signs. Say them to yourself when you wake in the morning and when you lie down at night, and when you wake in the middle of the night. And whatever strange things may happen to you, let nothing turn your mind from following the Signs. . . . Here on the mountain I have spoken to you clearly: I will not often do so down in Narnia. Here on the mountain, the air is clear and your mind is clear; as you drop down into Narnia, the air will thicken. Take great care that it does not confuse your mind. And the Signs which you have learned here will not look at all as you expect them to look, when you meet them there. That is why it is so important to know them by heart and pay no attention to appearances. Remember, remember the Signs and believe the Signs.[2]

"Thick air" causes believers to forget. We are like a man who looks at himself in the mirror and then forgets what he sees (Jas 1:22-24). Knowing this tendency, the Lord commanded the king of Israel to "write for himself in a book a copy of [the] law," keeping it close at hand and reading from it "all the days of his life," so that he will not drift from God's righteous commands (Deut 17:18-20).

---

[2]Ibid., 21.

Scripture consistently portrays God as remembering. Being made in the image of God, we have a similar capacity. Thus memory is a gift and an opportunity for stewardship. When we utilize only rudimentary memory, we operate more like animals than humans. Animals have enough memory to return to their nests and avoid dangerous areas based on past experience, but they lack the capacities of language, reason, and will required to put memories to use toward ethical and spiritual purposes.

The Bible is replete with characters who do not utilize the full range of memory. For example, the unjust steward in Jesus' parable forgets that his own enormous debt has been forgiven and refuses to show mercy to an acquaintance who owes him a small sum (Mt 18:23-35). Likewise, King David forgets that the Lord lifted him from a low estate—the youngest son of a shepherd—and shows no mercy to another man of lower status. Then Nathan stirs David's memory with a parable and admonition (2 Sam 12:7-9). The nation of Israel fails to remember how God delivered them from slavery: "They forgot God, their Savior, who had done great things in Egypt" (Ps 106:21). Forgetting God leads the people to worship idols, and that pattern of apostasy occurs repeatedly throughout the period of the Judges. They lapse into idolatry because they do "not remember the LORD their God" (Judg 8:34).

Forgetfulness is a problem for Jesus' disciples too. When the Twelve travel with Jesus across the Sea of Galilee and forget to bring bread, they think Jesus' warning about the "leaven of the Pharisees and Sadducees," is a rebuke for that lapse. But they have actually forgotten something more important—the miracle of feeding the five thousand (Mt 16:9-12). Their spiritual dullness muddles their understanding of Jesus' words, and they're unable to make the connections he intends. Conversely, after Jesus' resurrection the disciples remember their master's teaching about his passion so that they understand more fully the character of God's Messiah and the kingdom he would bring (Jn 2:22; 12:16; 16:4).

NEUROSCIENCE: FEARFULLY
AND WONDERFULLY MADE

The children of the covenants, both old and new, tend to forget. One reason we do so is simply because of the way the brain operates. Your brain is about the size of a head of cauliflower. It looks and feels like a three-and-a-half pound lump of firm tofu.[3] It makes up about 2 percent of your body's mass, but it uses 20 percent of the body's energy as it hums, whirrs, pulses, and purrs. Breathtakingly complex, this "tofu" is capable of amazing achievements.

In the 1920s, a Russian mnemologist named Solomon Shereshevskii performed staggering feats of memory on stage.[4] He was so remarkable that Aleksandr Luria, a leading psychologist, studied him over a period of thirty years. Shereshevskii could recall strings of more than a hundred digits, long strings of nonsense syllables, poetry in unknown languages, and elaborate scientific formulae. The key to these accomplishments? Imagery. Shereshevskii created a vast mental repository of visual images using "synesthesia," or a blending of the senses. For example, when subjected to a sound of two thousand cycles per second, Shereshevskii described his experience like this: "It looks something like fireworks tinged with a pink-red hue. The strip of colour feels rough and unpleasant, and it has an ugly taste—rather like that of a briny pickle."[5]

Memory is a function of the brain's hundred billion neurons, or nerve cells.[6] Neurons have a thin, complicated shape like the branch of a tree. These cells can be as short as a millimeter or as long as a meter. At one end is the axon and at the other end are dendrites, the twigs on the branch. Neurons communicate with each other by

---

[3] An excellent layman's introduction to neuroscience with applications for ministry is Bob Sitze, *Your Brain Goes to Church: Neuroscience and Congregational Life* (Herndon, VA: Alban Institute, 2005). Much of the material of this section is summarized from pages 5-9.

[4] Alan Baddeley, *Your Memory: A User's Guide* (New York, Macmillan, 2004), 44-45.

[5] Ibid., 45.

[6] Researchers actually don't know how many neurons the brain possesses and estimates range widely—from ten billion to two hundred billion. Most sources present the larger estimates—at least one hundred billion—as accurate.

sending chemical and electrical signals racing down the branch at two hundred miles an hour. When the charge reaches the end of the cell it leaps the "synapse"—the space between the dendrite and the next twiggy branch. Each cell is surrounded by ten to one hundred thousand dendrites, creating the possibility of one million billion possible connections. If we compare these synapses to a microprocessor, one human brain has more switches than all the computers, routers, and Internet connections on earth. You can see that the brain is complex if not unfathomable. The phrase "fearfully and wonderfully made" is indeed apt.

From a neuroscience perspective, memory is the repeated firing of specific combinations of neurons. When a neural net fires together a few times, the memory is "short-term," and when the net fires repeatedly in the same sequence, the memory moves to "long-term," giving rise to a neuroscience proverb: "Neurons that fire together wire together."[7] Scientists Aamodt and Wang describe the firing not like a computer with sequential linear processing, but more like a busy restaurant: "it's crowded and chaotic, and people are running around to no apparent purpose, but somehow everything gets done in the end."[8]

Using a different comparison, Horstman states, "It's tempting to think of memories as bits of sequential information stored in a specific place, rather like the love letters in an old shoebox, that you can just retrieve at will. However, your memories are not held neatly inside molecules or neurons."[9] Rather, when electrochemical signals are repeatedly sent down the same chain of long cells in the brain, leaping the tiny gaps between cells, the process becomes more efficient, a fixed pattern—a memory is formed. The more the neurons fire together, networking with multiple parts of the brain, the firmer the memory becomes.

---

[7]Sitze, *Your Brain Goes to Church*, 7.
[8]Sandra Aamodt and Sam Wang, *Welcome to Your Brain: Why You Lose your Car Keys but Never Forget How to Drive and Other Puzzles of Everyday Life* (New York: Bloomsbury, 2008), 22.
[9]Judith Horstman, *The Scientific American Brave New Brain* (San Francisco: Jossey-Bass, 2010), 39.

Remembering is a complicated whole-brain activity. It can originate in various parts of the brain such as the visual cortex, the
center where smell is processed, or the limbic system (a complex set
of brain structures that support emotion), all of which are coordi-
nated by the hippocampus. It is possible to change the brain physically when an act of learning grows new dendrites, but even if a
memory is long-term—that is, even if something has been learned
thoroughly—it needs to be refreshed. Memories fade like ink aging
on a handwritten letter.

Neuroscientists use the term "engramming" to describe the electrochemical process we call remembering. An engram is a kind of
pathway in the brain created when we have new experiences or receive
new information. These pathways become "memory traces," and all
information that follows is overlaid on these traces. I discovered this
process when a tennis coach tried to get me to hit my forehand with
more topspin. It wasn't pretty. My brain begged me to stay with the
tried-and-true engram, my flat and ineffectual stroke.

Engramming also helps explain why we instinctively harmonize
new information with old. The information may contradict the old,
but we do not easily let go of what we think we know. Engrams offer
a pathway over which impulses can travel easily.[10] Neural networks
that have fired and wired together harmonize new material and ignore
other material if it does not fit the existing perception of reality. In
psychology these habituated patterns are called "schemata" or
"frames"—mental structures of preconceived ideas on which to organize knowledge of the world. Schemata help us not only to organize
new information but also to perceive it. People are more likely to
notice things that fit into their schemata, and they reinterpret or
distort contradictions to make them fit.[11]

---

[10]Richard Cox, *Rewiring Your Preaching: How the Brain Processes Sermons* (Downers Grove, IL: InterVarsity Press, 2012), 58.
[11]The concept of "schema" is standard fare in social and cognitive psychology. See Susan T. Fiske and Shelley E. Taylor, *Social Cognition*, 2nd ed. (New York: McGraw-Hill, 1991), chapters 4 and 5; and David C. Rubin, *Memory in Oral Traditions: The Cognitive Psychology of Epic, Ballads, and Counting-Out Rhymes* (Oxford: Oxford University Press, 1995), chapter 2.

Schemata are necessary to everyday life so that we can react to bits of data, not pause to analyze them. When you see a blinking light on the right fender of the car in front of you, you know the car will turn right. But it could also represent something outside that schema, such as a faulty taillight or a motorist who is unaware that the turn signal is active. We are generally well-served by our structures, but we must stay open to exceptions. If a man rises from the dead, how will your schemata handle that?

Another layer of complexity in understanding the brain's neurobiology arises because our minds are incapable of paying attention to all the sensory input they receive. To do so would drive us to distraction, so the brain filters the data, allowing into consciousness only that which matters. The reticular activating system (RAS) filters more than 99 percent of the sensory data it receives. What does the RAS allow? Novelty, movement, and surprise can garner short-term attention, but preachers want something deeper—engagement—and that occurs only through relevance. The brain is hardwired to help us survive, so it scans the horizon for danger and threat, safety and reward. We find it nearly impossible to give attention for an extended period of time to anything that seems irrelevant.

Because the brain attends to only a very small percentage of possible stimuli, when two people observe the same phenomenon, their brains are not necessarily paying attention to and retaining the same facts. Yet both brains produce a coherent account. That account is more like a collage than a picture as it combines bits of data into a portrayal of reality. This is why eyewitness accounts of the same event can differ markedly.[12]

Given the discoveries from neuroscience about perception and memory, researcher Steven Novella warns, "Far from being a passive recording of events, memory is constructed, filtered through our beliefs, and subjected to contamination and morphing over time. . . . It's naive to implicitly trust our memories. . . . Without external, objective

---

[12]In psychology this phenomenon is called the "Rashomon effect" from the 1950 film *Rashomon* by Akira Kurosowa, a brilliant exploration of perception and memory.

verification, we can't know how accurate the details of our memories are."[13] Memory is like a patchwork quilt. Some bits of cloth are selected and some are discarded, then the craftsman makes a coherent whole from the bits.

A striking biblical example of "contamination and morphing over time" is the story of the bronze serpent. The Lord directed Moses to create a piece of metalwork when fiery serpents came "among the people, and they bit the people, so that many people of Israel died" (Num 21:6). But the God of Israel made a way out: whoever would look at the bronze serpent set on a pole would live. The Israelites preserved this piece of craftsmanship for centuries and apparently stories and legends grew around it so that by the time of King Hezekiah it had become an idol. Archeology has discovered many other bronze or copper serpents in the ancient Near East, so it's possible that Israel adopted the ways of its pagan neighbors. Israel made offerings to the statue, but Hezekiah did what was right in the eyes of the Lord. Along with other idols, he "broke in pieces the bronze serpent that Moses had made" (2 Kings 18:4). Novella could be commenting on the phenomenon of the bronze serpent when he states, "We don't recall memories as much as we reconstruct and update them."[14] We harmonize and even invent details to make a memory harmonious with our currently held perceptions and beliefs.

In an experiment in 1932, researcher Frederic Bartlett asked British people to read a Native American folk tale called "The War of the Ghosts" and then had them retell it several times in the following year.[15] Bartlett demonstrated that listeners' beliefs—their schemata—influenced their interpretation and memory of the story. In particular, all the participants altered details to omit the story's supernaturalism because it did

---

[13]Steven Novella, *Your Deceptive Mind: A Scientific Guide to Critical Thinking Skills* (Chantilly, VA: Teaching Company, 2012), 28.

[14]Ibid., 1.

[15]F. C. Bartlett, *Remembering: A Study in Experimental and Social Psychology* (Cambridge: Cambridge University Press, 1932). Summarized in various sources including Lisa Washington Lamb, *Blessed and Beautiful: Multiethnic Churches and the Preaching that Sustains Them* (Eugene, OR: Cascade, 2014), 107; and Baddeley, *Your Memory*, 38-39.

not harmonize with their presuppositions. The subjects muted or amplified parts of the story in ways that reflected their own worldview.

Oral communication tends to evolve, as you may remember from playing the telephone game in which one person whispers a story into the ear of her neighbor, who then whispers it to the next person, and so forth. By the time the last person in the chain tells the story, you may not recognize the original! In contrast to oral communication, shifting and ephemeral, written communication is stable, so God has inscripturated the Word. He has given us a written account of the master plan of redemption that keeps our memories and traditions on the path of truth.

Another form of communication, visual symbols such as altars, stones of remembrance, the Passover, and the Lord's Supper, are powerful aids to memory but are also potentially ambiguous. Thus these nonverbal communications are best combined with verbal communication—exposition of what the symbols mean. Material that has been learned must be refreshed in new contexts. Repetition is necessary, and multiple modes of instruction—verbal, experiential, artistic—greatly enhance both learning and retention.

MEDIA: THE WORLD IS TOO MUCH WITH US

Another barrier to remembering is the influence of media on our thinking—not on *what* we think (that's a topic for another book) but *how* we think. The human mind conforms to the medium through which it receives information. Our brains want to choose the path of least resistance, so when neural pathways—engrams—constantly fire and wire together, we become adept at using those pathways while others atrophy. Consider the medium of print, the one you are experiencing right now. You are using one sense (sight) to decipher abstract, arbitrary symbols (letters and punctuation). Although the act of reading raises no eyebrows—after all, we have been reading since early childhood—the phenomenon is actually enormously complicated. Only the human brain can handle it. In an amazing feat of alchemy, our brains transform arbitrary strokes and dots and dashes on a page into concepts, and the engramming makes us skilled at abstract, analytical, silent, private thinking.

Electronic communication, starting with the telegraph, is producing its own kind of "readers." I put that word in quotation marks because reading today is becoming nonlinear. For thousands of years reading required the eyes to move sequentially from left to right along lines and from top to bottom along pages, but new media encourage the eyes to skim and scan. This kind of "reading," perhaps most prevalent when we're reading on the Internet, corresponds to the changes we're seeing in visual media. For example, in old black-and-white movies, the camera was static, creating the impression of watching a play from a fixed seat in the theater. Today, multiple camera angles, jump cuts, and nonsequential storytelling demand a different set of skills to understand and enjoy film.

The changes in our reading habits reflect engramming that is comfortable with fragmentation and speed. Fewer people are choosing to read lengthy pieces that demand sustained concentration. Texting and tweeting are the name of the game. Sound bites and eye bytes rule the airwaves. Our culture is becoming "aliterate," a term suggested by James Billington, the librarian of Congress in 2009.[16] Aliterates can read (they're not illiterate), but reading in the electronic world forms a new kind of brain comfortable only with brevity and addicted to distraction. Seventeen percent of website page views last less than four seconds, whereas only 4 percent last more than ten minutes. When a web page is short (fewer than 112 words), readers read 49 percent of the words. When the web page is long (more than 593 words) Internet users read 28 percent of the content. As the word count increases, the average reader spends an extra 4.4 seconds for each increase of one hundred words.[17] Electronic media are making us adept at skimming and inept at exegeting.

---

[16]T. David Gordon, *Why Johnny Can't Preach: The Media Have Shaped the Messengers* (Phillipsburg, NJ: P&R, 2009), 37.

[17]"Attention Span Statistics," Statistic Brain, July 2, 2016, www.statisticbrain.com/attention-span-statistics.

In 2015, when the prestigious Oxford Dictionary named its "word of the year," it wasn't a word. It was an emoji, a pictograph of a yellow smiley face shedding tears of joy. The president of Oxford Dictionaries stated, "Traditional alphabet scripts have been struggling to meet the rapid-fire, visually focused demands of 21st Century communication. . . . A pictographic script like emoji has stepped in to fill those gaps."[18] Today's "readers" prefer script that conveys content and tone holistically rather than sequentially as with traditional lines of print.

As modern media shape the way we read, they are actually shaping something larger—perception and attention.[19] We live in a vast ecosystem of interruption, a bite-sized culture where phones jiggle and jingle with incoming messages. Even when we give sustained attention to activities like playing video games, and even when we engage in activities that require the use of words such as texting, we use portions of the brain that privilege speed, efficiency, brevity, and immediacy. Such technologies tend to create minds that have trouble holding still. Such a mind wants to be "distracted from distraction by distraction."[20]

Cultural critics such as Neil Postman began decrying the effects of electronic media even before the rise of the Internet. In 1985 he warned:

> There is no murder so brutal, no earthquake so devastating, no political burden so costly—for that matter, no ball score so tantalizing or weather report so threatening—that it cannot be erased from our minds by the newscaster saying, "Now . . . this." The newscaster means that you have thought long enough on the previous matter (approximately forty-five seconds), that you must not be morbidly preoccupied with it (let us say, for ninety seconds).[21]

---

[18]Mark Molloy, "An Emoji Was Named the Oxford Dictionaries Word of the Year and People Want to Leave Planet Earth," *The Telegraph*, November 2015, www.telegraph.co.uk/news /newstopics/howaboutthat/12000092/An-emoji-was-named-the-Oxford-Dictionaries -Word-of-the-Year-and-people-want-to-leave-planet-Earth.html.

[19]Nicholas G. Carr, *The Shallows: What the Internet Is Doing to Our Brains* (New York: W. W. Norton, 2010), 115-43.

[20]T. S. Eliot, Four Quarters, Book 1, "Burnt Norton," III. l. 101, www.coldbacon.com/poems /fq.html.

[21]Neil Postman, *Amusing Ourselves to Death: Public Discourse in the Age of Show Business* (New York: Penguin, 1985), 99-100.

The engramming that takes place through constant exposure to fragments makes our minds fall into a nervous search for new stimuli. Even when we are away from our screens, our minds continue to click around. These minds are dominated by *curiositas*, the things that tempted pilgrims to drift from the goal of their journey by gawking at novelties along the way. It is the stimulated but uninvolved gaze of the tourist.

Postman and other critics built on the writings of Marshal McLuhan, the patriarch of modern media studies, who spoke in 1962 about "media fall-out,"[22] a striking image coined in the Cold War era. The effects of media mushroom outward to influence how we think and behave. The blast may not kill us, but the fallout can work its own silent death. One thing that dies is memory. McLuhan and Postman are well-known modern proponents of the argument that media shape epistemology. The notion, however, is as old as Plato. In ancient Greece, a primarily oral culture, proponents of the new medium of writing touted it as an aid to memory, but Plato took the opposite view:

> This invention will produce forgetfulness in the souls of those who have learned it. They will not need to exercise their memories, being able to rely on what is written, calling things to mind no longer from within themselves by their own unaided powers, but under the stimulus of external marks. . . . So, it's not a recipe for memory.[23]

Plato's point was similar to the one made by modern scholars of media ecology—the form of communication influences how we think.

Vast storage capabilities and instantaneous transmission lead to information overload, what Edna St. Vincent Millay called "a meteoric shower of facts."[24] It becomes impossible to discern what should be

---

[22] Marshall McLuhan, *The Gutenburg Galaxy* (Toronto: University of Toronto Press, 1962), 246.

[23] Plato, *Phaedrus*, trans. W. C. Helmold and W. G. Rabinowitz (Indianapolis: Library of Liberal Arts, 1956), 68.

[24] Edna St. Vincent Millay, *Collected Sonnets* (New York: Harper, 1988), 140. The term "information overload" was originally coined by Alvin Toffler back in the 1970s as a warning about embracing the new technologies. The term gained broad currency in discussions of psychological disorders, attention deficit, and productivity problems associated with processing

retained and what discarded. In the electronic age, information exists for distraction and entertainment but not wisdom, for who can discern what bits are worth keeping to help us live successfully in the fear of God? Who can sift the grain from the chaff? On the same screen we can surf through death in the Middle East, a love story filmed sixty years ago, the latest advance in cancer research, scores of ballgames happening in real time, and a commercial for toothpaste that promises a dazzling smile, all within a few seconds. The montage and barrage of images, stories, facts, and opinions dampens our ability to differentiate, flattening all information into a thin veneer of entertainment. Wireless Woman and Media Man may know everything about the last twenty-four hours, but how much do they know about the last twenty-four centuries? Wisdom and shalom demand memory, the stockpiling and heeding of our forebears' experience. Media saturation helps us process information but not understand or reflect on it.

Electronic media create a culture that challenges memory, but the human heart creates an even deeper, internal challenge. In the words of John Calvin, the human heart is a "factory of idols."[25]

THE HEART: PRONE TO WANDER, LORD I FEEL IT

The faith journey of Charles Darwin brings to mind the warning of Hebrews 2:1: "We must pay much closer attention to what we have heard, lest we drift away from it." The great scientist was brought up in a conventionally Christian home in Victorian England, accepted the veracity of the Bible and the church's creeds, and after rejecting medicine as a career, considered the ministry as another gentlemanly profession. While traveling the world as a naturalist aboard the HMS *Beagle*, Darwin became convinced that species developed by chance over vast epochs of time. That belief eventually led him to reject the

---

vast amounts of information. See Alvin Toffler, *Future Shock* (New York: Bantam Books, 1984).

[25]John Calvin, *Institutes of the Christian Religion*, ed. John T. McNeill, trans. F. L. Battles (Louisville: Westminster John Knox, 1960), 108.

Genesis account as divinely inspired and eventually the whole Old
Testament. Then he rejected the Gospels because of their accounts of
miracles and the discrepancies in the supposedly eyewitness records.
Then a severe personal storm caused him to drift further—the death
of his dear daughter Annie when she was only ten years old.

Although the great scientist never became an outright atheist, his
belief in God slowly evolved into something like the deist's "first cause."
Commenting on this slow drift, one of Darwin's biographers says,
"Just as his clerical career had died a slow 'natural death,' so his faith
had withered gradually."[26] In Darwin's own words, "I gradually came
to disbelieve in Christianity as a divine revelation. . . . I was very un-
willing to give up my belief . . . but I found it more and more difficult
. . . to invent evidence which would suffice to convince me. Thus dis-
belief crept over me at a very slow rate, but was at last complete. The
rate was so slow that I felt no distress."[27]

Forgetting God is tantamount to forsaking him to worship idols,
and we are prone to do just that. Isaiah makes the link between
idolatry and forgetting in chapter 57. Judah has poured out drink offerings and brought grain offerings to idols, yet the nation still keeps
the outward trappings of true worship as prescribed in the law. They
have a form of obedience but not the substance. In particular, they still
retain the "memorial" in their houses—the words of the Shema (Deut
6:4-5)—but they place it "behind the door and the doorpost" (Is 57:8),
out of sight and out of mind. They retain a hypocritical show of obedience, but in fact their religion is syncretistic. They do not remember
the Lord (Is 57:11).

A specific form of idolatry is serving mammon, which seems to
exert a perennial, magnetic attraction on humans (see Mt 6:24; Col
3:5). When Israel is ready to enter the Promised Land, Moses sees
days of prosperity coming, so he warns them to not forget the Lord.
In particular, he singles out the numbing effects of material prosperity

---

[26]James Moore, *The Darwin Legend* (Grand Rapids: Baker, 1994), 46.
[27]Charles Darwin, *Life and Letters of Charles Darwin* (New York: D. Appleton and Co., 1911),
    1:278.

on the human heart. An abundance of food, flocks, silver, and gold can cause them to forget the Lord their God, whispering deceptively: "My power and the might of my hand have gotten me this wealth" (Deut 8:11-18). C. S. Lewis might say that in the Promised Land, a land flowing with milk and honey, the atmosphere is thick. It fogs the mind.

Knowing the human propensity to forget God, Scripture warns, "Keep yourselves from idols" (1 Jn 5:21), and "Keep yourselves in the love of God" (Jude 21). One way we keep ourselves is with deliberate acts of memory. Memories seem to spring to mind with a will of their own, but in Scripture memory is usually intentional, a discipline involving reading and pondering Scripture, hearing expositions of the same, and engaging in rituals that recall God's acts of grace in the past in order to actualize them in the present and chart a course for the future. By remembering we renew our minds and strengthen ourselves in the Lord. By so doing, we keep ourselves in the love of God.

Although we have a propensity to make idols all on our own, we are also influenced toward forgetfulness by the world. The lust of the flesh, the lust of the eyes, and the pride of life crowd out the seed planted in good soil. That's what Jesus taught his followers in the parable of the seed and soils (Mk 4:1-20). The thorns represent the cares of the world, or, in Jesus' words, "the deceitfulness of riches and the desires for other things" (Mk 4:19). When the smothering influence of the world focuses our attention on pleasure, achievement, and acquisition, we forget God.

Against the propensity to forget, God gives his followers story, that is, historical narrative. The Christian faith, as well as the Jewish, is grounded in history. We do not follow cleverly devised fables but rather the Word made flesh who was born of the Virgin Mary, suffered under Pontius Pilate, died, was buried, and rose again. The cross (and the exodus) happened in space and time. Thus, preachers in the Bible such as Moses, the prophets, and the apostles reminded their auditors again and again of facts historical and facts theological. The two cannot, or at least should not, be separated.

David's well-stocked storehouse of memories of how God delivered him in the past provided all the wares he needed for spiritual armor as he prepared to fight Goliath: "The LORD who delivered me from the paw of the lion and from the paw of the bear will deliver me from the hand [the Hebrew word is "paw"] of this Philistine" (1 Sam 17:34-37). Remembrance of God's power in the past gave David courage to act in the present.

The historical event of remembrance par excellence in the Old Testament is the exodus. God constantly reminds the Hebrew people of their bondage in Egypt, deliverance through the Red Sea, disobedience in the wilderness, and establishment in the land.[28] As we saw in chapter one, biblical memory of historical events is not just mental recall—it is participation. When ministers serve as remembrancers, reminding covenant children of the exodus, they enable that participation.

PROPER FORGETTING

While the Bible depicts forgetting mostly in dire terms related to apostasy, it also presents some instances when it is a blessing. We should forget some things.

We do not want to be like the fifty-five individuals in the United States who have been diagnosed with hyperthymesia, also known as highly superior autobiographical memory (HSAM).[29] These people spend an excessive amount of time thinking about their past and display extraordinary ability to recall specific events. Alexandre Wolfe is one of the fifty-five. In an interview with National Public Radio, she describes how she remembers every detail of a mundane activity like

---

[28]A sampling from just two books of the Hebrew Bible demonstrates how frequently the authors recall the exodus: Deut 1:27, 30; 4:9-14, 20-24, 33, 37, 45-46; 5:6, 15; 6:12, 20-25; 7:6-8, 15, 17-19; 8:2-4, 14-16; 9:6-29; 10:19, 22; and Ps 44, 66, 68, 74, 77, 78, 80, 81, 95, 99, 103, 105, 106, 114, 136. This emphasis continues in the New Testament in passages such as 1 Cor 10:1-13 and Heb 12:18-22.

[29]Alix Spiegel, "When Memories Never Fade, the Past Can Poison the Present," National Public Radio, December 27, 2015, www.wbur.org/npr/255285479/when-memories-never -fade-the-past-can-poison-the-present.

driving to Target for groceries that occurred more than ten years ago. She remembers what she wore and ate every day for the past decade. She remembers if the fan in the bedroom was running on this date last year. For her, memory is "almost like time travel" where she relives the past in concrete detail. Sometimes this extraordinary ability is an advantage, but at other times—many other times—it is a curse. Another interviewee says he remembers all the wrongs done against him and all the wrongs he has committed. He is haunted and harassed by those memories, demonstrating, as the NPR story states, that "we need to forget as much as we need to remember."[30]

Keeping in mind that forgetting in the Bible is volitional, disciples of Jesus exercise the spiritual discipline of no longer focusing on the past. Disciples must forget the world. "No one who puts his hand to the plow and looks back is fit for the kingdom of God" (Lk 9:62). Lot's wife looked back to gaze at the city of destruction and was destroyed (Gen 19:26). In contrast, Abraham and Sarah accepted their position as strangers and exiles on earth. They did not look back because they desired "a better country, . . . a heavenly one" (Heb 11:13-16). The old chorus summarizes the stance disciples take toward the world: "I have decided to follow Jesus . . . no turning back, no turning back."

Disciples should also forget forgiven sins. I'm not suggesting a cavalier or callous scoffing at past sins, because psychological freedom comes only when one has remembered those sins and repented. Dante pictures this in *The Divine Comedy*. As the narrator treks to paradise, he must first pass through purgatory, and on the border between the two realms he comes to a spring that divides into two streams, the river of forgetfulness and the river of memory.[31] Before drinking from the Lethe, the river of forgetfulness, the narrator must first remember his sins because neither river operates without the other. The narrator's guide, presumably Lady Wisdom, forces him to listen to an accounting of his sins and then to look at himself in the river. He weeps

---

[30]Ibid.
[31]Dante, *The Divine Comedy*, trans. Louis Biancolli (New York: Washington Square, 1968), 282-97.

at what he sees. Only then does the guide say, "Hold on to me!" as she plunges him under the water to drink from the river of forgetfulness. Thus bathed, he emerges into overwhelming light, a foretaste of paradise, the next and final stage of his journey. Memory makes us weep at our sins, which leads to repentance, and repentance leads to cleansing.

Because of the grace of God extended in Christ, believers can forget their forgiven sins. When the accuser of the brothers (Rev 12:10) impugns God's character and wrecks the believer's hope by parading sins through the halls of memory, those believers should turn a "blind eye and deaf ear" to the accusations. That was Spurgeon's advice to his students.[32] One blind eye and one deaf ear can be quite handy at times. When praised overmuch, listen with your deaf ear, and when accused of forgiven sins, view them with your blind eye. Emily Dickinson said something similar, musing that memory is like a house. It has rear and front porches and a "garret," an attic. That's where "the mouse" and some memories belong—out of sight and out of mind.[33]

The Russian mnemologist Shereshevskii needed a garret. His gift created a problem—he remembered too many things. His mind was cluttered. Eventually he hit on a simple solution: he imagined the information he wished to forget written on a blackboard, and then he imagined himself rubbing it out. Strangely enough, this method worked perfectly to declutter his house of remembrance.[34] That's what we should do with confessed sin.

The "Zeigarnik effect" helps explain why we remember our failures. In brief, people remember interrupted and unfinished tasks better than completed ones. The brain desires closure, but mistakes register in the brain as unfinished tasks ("When he accused me, I should have said, 'I'm sorry.' Instead I blew up! I've confessed my sin, but I can't shake the guilt feelings!"). The brain keeps such a program running in the background (to borrow a computer metaphor) until the task is

[32]C. H. Spurgeon, *Lectures to My Students* (Grand Rapids: Baker, 1977), 163-78.
[33]Emily Dickinson, *The Complete Poems of Emily Dickinson*, ed. Thomas H. Johnson (Boston: Little, Brown, 1960), 524-25.
[34]Baddeley, *Your Memory*, 44-45.

finished. Thus, like Hamlet's ghost, past sins haunt the hallways of the mind. The cure is to make a full confession to God and the person wronged, make appropriate restitution where possible, and then turn your attention away from your own actions—both the sin and the repentance—to the declaration of the one who forgives: "In Christ Jesus you who once were far off have been brought near by the blood of Christ" (Eph 2:13).

A final category of memories to forget is so-called accomplishments, especially those achievements by which we sought to impress God. Paul had plenty: he was "advancing in Judaism" beyond many of his own age and was "extremely zealous" for the traditions of his fathers (Gal 1:14). He was a "Hebrew of the Hebrews," a Pharisee who was blameless, but he forgot those accomplishments. All who are mature should think this way (Phil 3:5-15). When pride calls "achievement" to the witness stand to impress the Judge, disciples turn their backs. The blind eye and deaf ear come in handy once again.

A powerful tool to combat forgetting is speaking. Speech requires syntax and empathy, and both of those are complicated neural activities requiring sections of the brain to work together rather than allocating resources to the object causing fear.[35] Emergency workers seem to have discovered this through praxis. "Talk to me" is one of their first directives when starting to assist wounded and confused persons. Rehearsing aloud the covenantal promises of God through testimony, praise, prayer, and conversation causes neural pathways to fire that divert attention from haunting failures.

The psalms of lament illustrate the power of speaking aloud with their consistent pattern of complaint followed by hope and praise. Laments begin in doubt and discouragement but then hinge and turn 180 degrees. For example, in Psalm 77 Asaph moans and sighs because God almost seems to be his adversary. But then the poem shifts with these words: "Then I said, 'I will remember the deeds of the LORD'" (Ps 77:11). He engages in the discipline of remembering. He stops

---

[35]Sitze, *Your Brain Goes to Church*, 111.

listening to the chorus of voices accusing God and starts speaking
to himself:

> I will remember the deeds of the LORD;
>> yes, I will remember your wonders of old. . . .
>> What god is great like our God? (Ps 77:11, 13)

Memory takes the psalmist by the hand to show him the faithfulness
of God, which the psalmist then rehearses aloud.

Remembering can be tough for a harried brain in the age of distraction with an idol-making heart tempted by the world, but God has
provided help through the ministry of remembrancers. Word and
sacrament, verbal and nonverbal weapons of the Spirit, help the
children of God remember what they should remember and forget
what they should forget.

3

THE LORD'S REMEMBRANCERS

I am not an innovator

but a rediscoverer of forgotten goods

and I hope a remover of obtrusive bric-a-brac.

THORTON WILDER

We have to be continually reminded of what we believe.

Neither this belief [in Christian doctrine]

nor any other will automatically remain alive in the mind.

It must be fed. . . . Do not most people simply drift away?

C. S. LEWIS, *MERE CHRISTIANITY*

●

AWAKENINGS IS a thought-provoking film based on the book with the same title by Oliver Sacks, the doctor you will remember from the introduction of this book who worked with Jimmie. The movie follows the story of Leonard, played by Robert DeNiro, and Dr. Sayer, played by Robin Williams.[1] Leonard's neurological system began to fail when he was a teenager living in the Bronx in the late 1930s, and by the time he's twenty, he is paralyzed and catatonic, his limbs contorted and his

---

[1]*Awakenings,* directed by Penny Marshall (Hollywood: Columbia Pictures, 1990).

face a mask. But Dr. Sayers believes that behind the blank eyes is a living soul, so he studies, thinks, and experiments with Leonard, hoping for a miracle of medicine.

Then it happens: Dr. Sayers gives Leonard an extra-large dose of an experimental drug and falls asleep beside his bed waiting to see if there is any improvement. In the small hours of the morning Sayers wakes with a start to discover that Leonard is gone! Searching the silent corridors of the hospital, he finds Leonard at a table in the recreational room. On tiptoes Dr. Sayers approaches and the two make eye contact. The doctor sits at the table. Leonard offers a laborious smile and whispers, "It's quiet."

"It's late," Dr. Sayers replies. "Everyone's asleep."

With a twinkle in his eye Leonard replies, "I'm not asleep."

The doctor agrees: "No, you're awake." Leonard has been scratching his name on paper with a crayon and the doctor asks to see what he is writing. With the twinkle again, Leonard announces: "Me!"

We might take this moving scene as a parable for the work of a remembrancer. In the Spirit's power, the preacher awakens believers who then remember their identity: they are children of God, joint heirs with Christ, a royal priesthood, and redeemed with a price. The lights go on and they assert: "Me!"

That's what happened to my friend who had drifted from God. Estranged from her husband and children, she was living in the far country like the prodigal. But then she found herself in church watching a drama of a woman who also dwelt in that country. With tears of remorse and hope, my friend awoke to remember her true identity. When remembrancers minister as instruments of the Spirit, they have the joy of seeing lights go on, conscience stir, hope revive, and behavior change.

STIRRING MEMORY: PREACHING
LIKE PREACHERS IN THE BIBLE

Stirring memory is one of the minister's primary tasks. In a sense, all biblical preaching in the context of a worship service is an act of reminding.[2] Theologian John Davis states that when the church re-enacts the story of redemption through preaching, Scripture reading, and sacrament, the assembly experiences "sacred time travel" as they are re-membered to the cross, resurrection, and ascension.[3]

Ministers might ask how "sacred time travel" ensues when the preacher tells the old, old story. Theologically and rhetorically, the answer is that God's words do things; they have "performative power." Just as the statement "I pronounce you husband and wife" enacts the thing it names, so do God's words accomplish what they state. When God said, "Let there be light," there was light. And when the Lord Jesus said, "This cup that is poured out for you is the new covenant in my blood," a new covenant came to be. The Word is a lamp that illumines, a fire that consumes, a hammer that breaks stony hearts, a sword that pierces, water that cleanses, a seed that bears fruit, a mirror that reveals, and milk that nourishes. When ministers preach God's powerful Word as faithful stewards, their words have a derivative power that accomplishes God's will through the power of the Spirit.

Thus, when a preacher faithfully re-presents redemptive history, worshipers see the hand of God smite the Egyptians on their behalf, part the Red Sea for their deliverance, and provide manna in the desert for them. They see the sun darkened and feel the ground shake when the greater Moses performs a greater deliverance at the cross. Believers stand at the empty tomb with the women to hear the angel say, "He is not here. He is risen." Stirred by a preacher, the listeners' memory becomes participation. The past is brought into the present with power, and action results. In short, God's Word, faithfully announced, builds faith.

---

[2] Approaching Christian preaching from a secular standpoint, communication scholar Michael C. McGee defines the genre of Christian "sermon" and concludes that the primary feature of the genre is "thematic reduplication." It moves deductively from an immutable premise derived from "ultimate authority" (the Bible) to a tautological restatement of that premise as exemplified in particular situations. "Thematic Reduplication in Christian Rhetoric," *Quarterly Journal of Speech* 56, no. 2 (1970): 196-204.

[3] John Jefferson Davis, *Worship and the Reality of God: An Evangelical Theology of Real Presence* (Downers Grove, IL: InterVarsity Press, 2010), 92.

To see what the work of a remembrancer looks like we need look no further than Scripture, which is replete with examples of preachers performing "sacred time travel." We will examine three preachers, or sets of preachers: Moses in Deuteronomy, the prophets, and the apostles in the Epistles.[4]

Deuteronomy: Remember and do not forget. The covenant people were poised to enter the Promised Land. Their forty years of wandering were done, and God was commissioning them to finish the task begun at the Red Sea: claiming the land. But the current generation had not seen the mighty acts of redemption in Egypt. They had not witnessed the Red Sea parting. They were not present when God made a covenant with their fathers at Sinai. Yet these people who stood at the Jordan River were subjects of the same God and participants in the same covenant as those who had stood at the Red Sea. Memory would actualize those facts.

Moses' farewell address to Israel recorded in Deuteronomy stresses repeatedly that the people must remember and not forget. What should be the objects of memory? Their slavery in Egypt (Deut 16:12; 24:22), their deliverance, often with wonders (Deut 5:15; 6:12; 7:18-19; 8:14; 15:15; 16:3; 24:18), the making of the covenant at Sinai (Deut 4:9-13, 23), Yahweh himself (Deut 4:39-40; 8:11, 14, 18, 19), the commandments (Deut 11:18; 26:13), their rebellion in the wilderness and God's discipline (Deut 8:2, 14-16; 9:7; 24:9), Amalek (Deut 25:17-19), and the days of old (Deut 32:7).

The prompting of memory occurred both verbally and nonverbally— that is, Moses preached to the people, and the people also participated in festivals, such as Passover and Booths, that were rich with sensory experience. We will return to the nonverbal mode in chapter seven, but here we note that ceremony was not devoid of verbal instruction— preaching, teaching, and especially public reading of Scripture. The

---

[4]These texts are great repositories of preaching as reminding, but many other passages carry out the same function. For example, see Psalm 78. The psalmist says that there are things he has heard and known from his fathers, and he is committed to passing on those things to the next generation and even to "the children yet unborn" who in turn will pass on the same stories and truths to the following generation.

regular reading of the law at the festivals reminded the people of their responsibilities to obey the covenant stipulations (see Deut 31:9-13).

The preaching of Moses often stirred memory. Notice how he conflates the generation that came out of Egypt with the current generation moving into Canaan:

> When your son asks you in time to come, "What is the meaning of the testimonies and the statutes and the rules that the LORD our God has commanded you?" Then you shall say to your son, "We were Pharaoh's slaves in Egypt. And the LORD brought us out of Egypt with a mighty hand. And the LORD showed signs and wonders, great and grievous, against Egypt and against Pharaoh and all his household, before our eyes. And he brought us out from there, that he might bring us in and give us the land that he swore to give to our fathers. And the LORD commanded us to do all these statutes, to fear the LORD our God, for our good always, that he might preserve us alive, as we are this day." (Deut 6:20-24)

> The Egyptians treated us harshly and humiliated us and laid on us hard labor. Then we cried to the LORD, the God of our fathers, and the LORD heard our voice and saw our affliction, our toil, and our oppression. And the LORD brought us out of Egypt with a mighty hand and an outstretched arm, with great deeds of terror, with signs and wonders. (Deut 26:6-9)

Moses' conflation of the current generation poised to cross the Jordan River with the past generation that came through the Red Sea is not simply a rhetorical strategy; it is an exposition of a theological fact. The people of God are one people. Preachers remind believers, including New Testament believers, that they were included in God's mighty miracles of the past. Moses not only conflates the past generation with the current one; he also gathers in future generations, "whoever is not here with us today" (Deut 29:15).[5]

Centuries later the psalmists continue the practice of fusing generations, as in Psalm 114:3-5, where the crossing of the Red Sea and

---

[5]Other portions of Scripture, such as Psalm 47, announce the future as present today.

the crossing of the Jordan, separated by forty years of time, are mentioned in the same breath as if they were one event. Those events are so present to the poet that he can address them as if they stood before him:

> The sea looked back and fled;
>   Jordan turned back. . . .
>
> What ails you, O sea, that you flee?
>   O Jordan, that you turn back?

The rhetorical situation Moses faced is similar to the one Christian preachers face today. We stand on the brink of full deliverance, but we too are separated from the great deeds of redemption accomplished by Christ Jesus. So Christians lean heavily on memory to keep hope alive and faith strong. Christian ceremonies and discourse, particularly the Lord's Supper, Scripture reading, and sermons, actualize the past with compelling power.

The prophets: Do you not know? Have you not heard? The prophets were remembrancers par excellence. They drummed a metronomic cadence of covenant stipulations, incentives, and warnings. In fact, their cadence was so uniform and unceasing that they flirted with monotony. The themes of God's goodness, law, and rightful ownership and the people's rebellion leading to judgment appear in book after book, text after text. Jeremiah reminds the people of the Ten Commandments (Jer 7:9), Habakkuk echoes Deuteronomy when he warns of foreign conquest for covenant breakers (Hab 1:5-11; Deut 28:49-51), and Amos, like Moses, conflates past and present: "[God] brought you up out of the land of Egypt and led you forty years in the wilderness" (Amos 2:10). The exodus, Sinai, and wilderness wanderings form a refrain the prophets never tire of repeating as they offer the message of deliverance, gratitude, and obligation.

At times these spokesmen for God reach back even further than the exodus, all the way back to the patriarchs, as in Isaiah 51:1-3, where the prophet comforts those who pursue righteousness. They will flourish again like Abraham and Sarah, who are described as "your father" and the one "who bore you." Isaiah also encourages the downtrodden with the account of Noah in Isaiah 54:9-11. Just as the flood came to an end, so will the exile. The covenant people receive strength for today and bright hope for tomorrow by remembering the work of God in the past.

Walter Brueggemann describes another ministry the prophets accomplished through memory—subverting the world's status quo. He states, "The empire, Babylonian or any other, wants to establish itself as absolute, wants the present arrangement to appear eternal."[6] After a while, subjects of the empire cannot remember when it was any different. This is why the prophets stepped in and spoke up with reminders of God's covenant made in the past, his presence even in exile, and his bright plan for the future. This helped the exiles remember their identity and stay true to the covenant. Brueggemann concludes, "Against such imperial absoluteness and positivism, memory can be a keenly subversive activity."[7] The prophets' rhetorical situation, like that of Moses, also parallels the task set before Christian preachers. God formed a covenant with Israel and then fulfilled that covenant in Christ for the church. Just as Israel lived under the stipulations of the first covenant, so the church lives under the stipulations of the second. All of God's people are to love and obey the king.

Epistles: By way of reminder. Like Moses and the prophets, Paul and the other New Testament letter writers regularly reminded their hearers of what they already knew and believed. The Epistles show what preaching to believers probably sounded like in the first century—not preaching for evangelism (Acts illustrates that), but preaching to the faith family within the walls of a house church. In such preaching we overhear the apostles stirring memory. Their Epistles show us that we are not forced to communicate something novel each week.

---

[6]Walter Brueggemann, *Hopeful Imagination: Prophetic Voices in Exile* (Philadelphia: Fortress, 1986), 112.
[7]Ibid.

STIRRING MEMORY IN THE EPISTLES

In the Epistles, readers are regularly reminded of the core tenets of the faith.

Romans 15:14-16. "I myself am satisfied about you, my brothers, that you yourselves are full of goodness, filled with all knowledge and able to instruct one another. But on some points I have written to you very boldly by way of reminder, because of the grace given me by God to be a minister of Christ Jesus to the Gentiles."

Jude 5, 17. "Now I want to remind you, although you once fully knew it, that Jesus, who saved a people out of the land of Egypt, afterward destroyed those who did not believe. . . . You must remember, beloved, the predictions of the apostles of our Lord Jesus Christ."

2 Peter 1:13-16. "I think it right, as long as I am in this body, to stir you up by way of reminder, since I know that the putting off of my body will be soon, as our Lord Jesus Christ made clear to me. And I will make every effort so that after my departure you may be able at any time to recall these things."

2 Peter 3:1-2. "This is now the second letter that I am writing to you, beloved. In both of them I am stirring up your sincere mind by way of reminder, that you should remember the predictions of the holy prophets and the commandment of the Lord and Savior through your apostles."

Ephesians 2:11-12. "Therefore remember that at one time you Gentiles in the flesh, called 'the uncircumcision' by what is called the circumcision, . . . remember that you were at that time separated from Christ."

Philippians 3:1-2. "Finally, my brothers, rejoice in the Lord. To write the same things to you is no trouble to me and is safe for you. Look out for the dogs, look out for the evildoers, look out for those who mutilate the flesh."

1 John 2:7. "Beloved, I am writing you no new commandment, but an old commandment that you had from the beginning."

Romans 6:3, 16; 11:2; 1 Corinthians 3:16, 5:6. "Do you not know . . . ?"

One of the Bible's great repositories of the ministry of reminding is Hebrews 11. The author lists a battery of Old Testament stories already known to his hearers to illustrate the robust nature of faith. Abel, Enoch, Noah, Abraham, Sarah, Isaac, Jacob, Joseph, the parents of

Moses, Moses himself—and on the list goes—demonstrate faith as the conviction of things not seen, a conviction that leads to action.

Similarly, to support the claim that "faith without works is dead," James alludes to the stories of Abraham and Rahab (Jas 2:20-26). He expects his audience to recognize the brief allusions, mentally fill in the details of the stories, and infer what he intends. When hearers collaborate with the author, helping him make his own case, they participate in their own persuasion. For instance, when James alludes to Abraham to argue that faith without works is dead, I can imagine his readers responding this way: "Let me recall the story you are alluding to, James—Abraham sacrificing Isaac. Oh yes! God said to him, 'Now I know you fear God. I will surely bless you because you have obeyed me.' Hmm. If Abraham had merely mouthed the right words but not acted on his faith, he would not have received God's blessing. Yes, James, you are right! Faith without works is useless. I see that real faith cannot be divorced from action." Allusion draws in the hearers, engages their minds and prompts them to collaborate in their own persuasion. This rhetorical dynamic is one of many that occur when preachers stir memory.

When the recipient of an epistle is himself a preacher, such as Timothy, we see a double act of reminding occurring. First the apostle Paul reminds Timothy of what he already knows, then he tells him to do the same for the believers under his charge. In 2 Timothy Paul heartens Timothy by letting him know that he remembers him in prayer (2 Tim 1:3) as he remembers Timothy's tears (2 Tim 1:4) and sincere faith, which was handed down from his grandmother and mother (2 Tim 1:4-5). Then Paul reminds Timothy to "fan into flame the gift of God" imparted through the laying on of hands (2 Tim 1:6). Timothy is to "follow the pattern of the sound words that you have heard from me" (2 Tim 1:13).[8]

After these personal memories and exhortations comes a reminder of doctrine, what Hughes and Chapell call the "grand essential

[8]Later in the epistle, the apostle will exhort Timothy to "continue in what you have learned and firmly believed" (2 Tim 3:14).

memory":[9] "Remember Jesus Christ, risen from the dead, the off-spring of David, as preached in my gospel" (2 Tim 2:8). This creedlike statement is a shorthand description of the whole gospel similar to 1 Corinthians 15:1-4 and Romans 1:1-4. The title "Jesus Christ, offspring of David" alludes to Jesus as the incarnated Son of God who is Messiah, and the brief phrase "risen from the dead" summarizes the deity of Christ vindicated by his Father in the resurrection. Furthermore, the word "risen" is in the perfect tense in Greek, indicating a past action with ongoing results. The resurrection assures believers that they too will rise (see also 1 Cor 15:20-22). After these personal and doctrinal recollections where Paul serves as a remembrancer for his beloved son, he says plainly, "Remind them of these things" (2 Tim 2:14). That's one of the primary things preachers do. They remind.

In addition to overt instances of stirring memory, the general structure of the Epistles also demonstrates that the apostles conducted themselves as remembrancers. I am referring to the well-known structure of indicative followed by imperative. When the Epistles command, rebuke, and exhort (the imperative), they do so on the basis of the character and work of God (the indicative). Jesus laid down his life for us (indicative), so we should lay down our lives for each other (imperative) (1 Jn 3:16-17). Because Jesus will bring departed saints with him when he comes again, we should not grieve like those who have no hope (1 Thess 4:13-18). Because Jesus became poor for us, we should give generously (2 Cor 8:8-12). In the Epistles, action is motivated by theology that has been brought to a burning focus in the minds of the recipients. Just as the Lord began the Decalogue with the indicative "I am the Lord who brought you out of Egypt" and then followed with moral exhortation—the Ten Commandments—the apostles stir memory of deliverance so the recipients will live in congruence with that deliverance. The proof of memory is fidelity.

---

[9]R. Kent Hughes and Bryan Chapell, *1 and 2 Timothy and Titus* (Wheaton, IL: Crossway, 2000), 201.

Memory actualizes latent knowledge and applies it to current circumstances. That is what we see in Moses, the prophets, and the apostles. They roused memory by preaching to the heart.

STIRRING MEMORY TARGETS THE HEART

In the Bible, the "heart" includes knowledge and belief—what we call "worldview"—and it also includes emotion. The old dichotomy between "head" and "heart," or "mind" and "emotion," does not come from the Bible.[10] In Holy Scripture the heart thinks (Prov 4:23; 23:7; Acts 8:22) and plans actions (Gen 6:5; Prov 16:1, 9), and it also experiences emotions such as joy (Deut 28:47), sorrow (1 Sam 1:8), anger (2 Kings 6:11), and anxiety (Jn 14:1). The Bible depicts the heart as an amalgamation of interior motives that lead to action, what the Puritans called "the affections." An accurate albeit awkward synonym for the biblical term "heart" is "motivational structure." From the confluence of perception, understanding, beliefs, values, and feelings, we are motivated to act.

It is possible to preach with exegetical accuracy but not reach the heart. Reminding may seem to be primarily a cognitive function of preaching, but it actually has just as much to do with emotion as cognition. This is because an act of reminding assumes that the listeners already know the content of an utterance, but their knowledge slumbers and must be aroused. It smolders and must be ignited.

That's what Fred Rogers ("Mr. Rogers" from the famous PBS children's show) did when he addressed the prestigious National Press Club in Washington, DC.[11] These lunches typically feature diplomats, administration officials, and opinion makers who address the top issues of the day, so members of the club thought they were in for a "light lunch" when Mr. Rogers came to town. They were in for a surprise.

---

[10]For a sustained argument about the inseparability of emotion and reason, see Samuel M. Powell, *The Impassioned Life: Reason and Emotion in the Christian Tradition* (Minneapolis: Fortress, 2016).

[11]This incident is recounted in Thomas G. Long, *Testimony: Talking Ourselves Into Being Christian* (San Francisco: Josey-Bass, 2004), 110.

Rogers began by taking out a pocket watch and announcing that he would conduct two minutes of silence. He instructed the group to remember people from their past—parents, coaches, friends, mentors, and so forth—who had made their success possible. Then he simply stood in silence, looking at his watch. The silence must have seemed eternal, but by the end, one reporter noticed the sounds of people sniffling and weeping softly as they remembered those who had loved them, made sacrifices for them, and given them gifts. The past was brought into the present with compelling power. When cognition and emotion work in tandem, memory can unscrew a tight lid.

Preaching as reminding captures interest, imagination, and emotion to reach the "motivational structure" from which people act. We want to preach to the whole person so that hearers are "cut to the heart" much like Peter's great sermon at Pentecost (Acts 2:37). The heart rests on what it believes to be true, rejoices in what it loves, and acts on what it worships. People do what they celebrate. Living faith arises when a preacher gives not only convincing proofs but also a compelling vision of splendors.

The man in Mark 9:16-29 illustrates the need to address the whole person. He already possessed some faith, for he believed enough to bring his spirit-tormented son to Jesus. Even so, an ache throbbed in his heart and confusion swirled in his mind: "I believe; help my unbelief!" That is where most parishioners need help, so the Lord's remembrancers step into the pulpit armed with the most convincing lines of reasoning and the most stirring emotions to build faith. By addressing the mind, will, and emotions, remembrancers speak to the heart.

Neuroscience affirms the inseparability of thinking and feeling.[12] Emotions occur when people or events promise us gain or loss, and thus emotions keep our minds focused on critical information that shapes behavior.[13] The mind attends to what it perceives as relevant for health, peace, security, and hope. Richard Cox, an expert in neuroscience

---

[12]Steven Novella, *Your Deceptive Mind: A Scientific Guide to Critical Thinking Skills* (Chantilly, VA: Teaching Company, 2012), 12.

[13]Sandra Aamodt and Sam Wang, *Welcome to Your Brain: Why You Lose your Car Keys but Never Forget How to Drive and Other Puzzles of Everyday Life* (New York: Bloomsbury, 2008), 100.

and an ordained minister, states, "The brain will not—and indeed cannot—occupy itself with unessential information. . . . Only what is essential to the preservation and enhancement of the person is entertained."[14] Thus bland and bald repetition of the great doctrines, like a scribe intoning the genealogies of North Umbria, will not reach the heart. The genealogies may be accurate and important, but the listener feels distanced from them, not re-membered to them. Such preaching does not build faith. The following chapters will suggest ways to stir faith in the pulpit.

RESPONDING TO CONCERNS

Perhaps my emphasis on emotion and the heart has raised red flags in your mind. Let's conclude this chapter by giving voice to some concerns that you may have. "What about reason?" you may ask. "Do you want us to bypass the mind and simply stir emotion? That sounds like modern advertising or demagoguery." These valid concerns deserve comment.

The role of reason. The choice between logos and pathos is not either-or but both-and. The affections must be anchored to truth, and truth must ride the wind of the affections. The most effective preaching is based on rigorous exegesis, and part of exegesis is understanding the flow of thought and argumentation used by the human (and divine) authors of each passage. The preacher explains, proves, and applies that original author's logos to a contemporary congregation, but logos should not be separated from pathos.

Jonathan Edwards faced the concern about the role of reason from the staid clergymen of Boston who felt that revivalistic preaching was only sound and fury signifying nothing. I appreciate Edwards's response, drawn from John 5:35:

> If the minister has light without heat . . . he may . . . fill the heads of his
> people with empty notions; but it will not be very likely to reach their

---

[14]Richard H. Cox, *Rewiring Your Preaching: How the Brain Processes Sermons* (Downers Grove, IL: InterVarsity Press, 2012), 74.

hearts, or save their souls. And if, on the other hand, he be driven on with . . . vehement heat, without light, he will be likely to kindle the like unhallowed flame in his people . . . but he will make them never the better, nor lead them a step towards heaven.[15]

At the risk of belaboring the point, allow me to state with conviction a short manifesto: sermons must use logos. They must not manipulate the emotions to bamboozle people into doing what their minds reject. Sermons must use evidence without spin and reason without dissimulation because the mind is an indispensable component of the heart. Logos is part of the ensemble of actors in the holistic drama of preaching, even though that particular actor is not in the spotlight in this book.

The role of teaching/explaining. As implied above, teaching is part of a minister's calling. The Great Commission includes teaching (Mt 28:20), and the apostle Paul was appointed as a teacher and preacher (2 Tim 1:11; 1 Tim 2:7) so that through "warning" and "teaching" he might "present everyone mature in Christ" (Col 1:28). The work of stirring memory is not antithetical to the work of teaching. In fact, the work of teaching depends on the work of reminding. The only way to teach anything unfamiliar is to move from the known to the unknown, so teachers start with the learner's field of experience and then move to the new term, concept, or process. For instance, skillful explanation of the term "Samaritan" to grade school children might use examples and analogies drawn from their world, such as a player on a rival sports team, a practitioner of a foreign religion who looks different, or even a cat who happens upon a dog. The teacher stirs knowledge and attitudes already present in the hearers (that is, he or she reminds them of what they know) and then bridges to the new thing.

As we can see, one of the best ways to explain anything new is with analogy—comparing the unknown to the known. Analogies can be as long as our Lord's parables, or even novel-length depictions of Jesus

[15]Jonathan Edwards, "The True Excellency of a Gospel Minister," *The Works of Jonathan Edwards*, 2:958, cited in John Piper, *The Supremacy of God in Preaching*, rev. ed. (Grand Rapids: Baker, 2004), 86.

as a lion (Aslan), or they can be as short as a word or phrase. We will return to the topic of analogy in the next chapter.

The role of apologetics and persuasion. Persuasion is also part of the minister's calling.[16] Apologist Os Guinness makes this case forcefully:

> The Bible . . . knows nothing of preaching divorced from the needed work of persuasion. The two words *preach* and *persuade*, and the two ideas behind them, are indissoluble—most prominently in the tireless work of St. Paul, who was an apologist everywhere he went. He preached and he persuaded. He persuaded and he preached, and no one can drive so much as the beam of a laser between the two.[17]

The apostle Paul, "knowing the fear of the Lord," sought to "persuade others" (2 Cor 5:11), so we see that persuasion is indeed one of the minister's jobs.

Like the art of teaching, which moves from the known to the unknown, the art of apologetics—indeed all persuasion—begins with the listener's presuppositions. Apologetics works with common grace to persuade someone to a new belief, summoning into the court of decision the knowledge God has engraved on each human heart. When apologetics is done well, Guinness says, those being persuaded are "hoist by their own petard."[18] A petard is an explosive device used to blow in a gate or breach a wall, and the verb "hoist" means to lift or raise. Thus the expression means to be hurt or destroyed by one's own device. For example, the relativist who claims with certainty that all truth is situational and perspectival can be confronted with his or her own certainty. The axiom "all truth is relative" is undermined by that very axiom.

Francis Schaeffer witnessed this in action when he was having tea in a student's room at Cambridge University. One guest from India, a Hindu, asserted that there is no difference between cruelty and

---

[16]R. Larry Overstreet, *Persuasive Preaching: A Biblical and Practical Guide to the Effective Use of Persuasion* (Wooster, OH: Weaver, 2014), 27-105.
[17]Os Guinness, *Fool's Talk: Recovering the Art of Christian Persuasion* (Downers Grove, IL: InterVarsity Press, 2015), 112.
[18]Ibid., 23-25, 119-20.

noncruelty—all is one. Of course, no one holds that belief consistently, so the student in whose room they met helped his guest see that. He picked up the steaming kettle of hot water and held it over the Indian's head who looked up and asked what he was doing. "With cold yet gentle finality, the host replied, 'There is no difference between cruelty and noncruelty.'" The Hindu student was hoist on his own petard and dropped the argument.[19] His own instinct arising from common grace led him to see that his assertion was not tenable. As George MacDonald said, "The best thing you can do for your fellow man, next to rousing his conscience, is—not to give him things to think about, but to wake things up that are in him; . . . to make him think things for himself."[20]

The principle of using the receiver's own beliefs and values has its roots in classical rhetoric's theory of the "enthymeme," which is a "rhetorical syllogism."[21] A standard syllogism is a closely reasoned argument with three statements:

- Major premise: All men are mortal.
- Minor premise: Socrates is a man.
- Conclusion: Therefore, Socrates is mortal.

This reasoning moves deliberately to an ironclad deduction.

In contrast to the syllogism, the enthymeme does not state one or two of the premises. Those ideas are still crucial to the argument, but if the audience already believes them, they can be left unstated. For example, because we already believe that all men are mortal, the persuader could simply argue, "Socrates is just a man. He's mortal!" and we would concur. A persuader could, in fact, jump straight to the conclusion, "Socrates is mortal," since we believe the major and minor premises even before they are spoken. Skillful rhetoricians analyze the audience to determine what beliefs and values they bring

[19]Francis Schaeffer, *The God Who is There,* vol. 1 of *The Complete Works of Francis Schaeffer* (Wheaton, IL: Crossway, 1933), 110.

[20]George MacDonald, *The Gifts of the Christ Child: Fairy Tales and Stories for the Childlike,* ed. Glenn Edward Sadler (Grand Rapids: Eerdmans, 1973), 1:27.

[21]Aristotle, *The Rhetoric and Poetics of Aristotle,* trans. W. Rhys Roberts (New York: Modern Library, 1954), 1356b.

to the table and then use those presuppositions to bring about change in the receivers.

Sometimes the rhetorician does this overtly by reminding the audience of their beliefs, and sometimes he or she does it subtly by prompting them to recall their own presuppositions, but in either case, the listeners end up collaborating with the persuader. In a sense, all persuasion is self-persuasion. Hearers must come to their own conclusions or else the so-called persuasion is actually manipulation or coercion. So when the Lord's remembrancers seek to persuade, they bring to the surface what the audience may have submerged. Skillful speakers awaken things already present to move the audience toward things absent.

The role of application and exhortation. The chief end of preaching is the conforming of the heart and behavior to the perfect will of God. This function of preaching overlaps with memory because wisdom—skillful living in the fear of God—draws on previously acquired knowledge to illumine a current situation and chart a course of behavior.

The angel's message to the church in Ephesus shows that memory is linked to action: "You have abandoned the love you had at first. Remember therefore from where you have fallen; repent, and do the works you did at first" (Rev 2:4-5). Similarly, to the church in Sardis: "You have the reputation for being alive, but you are dead. Wake up, and strengthen what remains and is about to die, for I have not found your works complete in the sight of my God. Remember, then, what you received and heard. Keep it, and repent" (Rev 3:1-3). You cannot keep what you do not hold, so a remembrancer gathers discarded memories and hands them again to careless believers. As we saw in the previous chapter, believers tend to drift, forgetting that they were "cleansed" from their sins (2 Pet 1:9). So a minister makes the past present once again, and the result is a revived heart with ensuing righteous actions.

Our post-Christian age of biblical illiteracy. In this post-Christian age, preachers have less common ground with listeners than they had in previous generations, so they must undertake the tasks of explaining, proving, and applying slowly and with patience by drawing on what common ground does exist. Self-disclosure, story, metaphor, and simile serve that goal well by tapping into shared experience and knowledge. For example, to teach the basic attributes of God to a congregation largely ignorant of that theology, the preacher could find analogies from common grace and experience: God is jealous like a mother dog protecting her pups; God will never leave us or forsake us, just as I stayed with my son when a tremendous thunderstorm broke; the memory capacity of the latest computer is nothing compared to the Lord's memory; the Lord's kingdom is breaking in just as the Allies' landing at Normandy began the long process of conquering evil and restoring freedom.

The role of Holy Spirit. Rather than assuming a dichotomy between the ministry of the Holy Spirit and the ministry of a human remembrancer, this book is grounded in a theology that asserts the necessity of both. Remembrance of Jesus' words, and by extension remembrance of the whole Bible (since all Scripture points to Christ—Lk 24:27), is animated by the Holy Spirit. Jesus says plainly in John 14:26, "The Helper, the Holy Spirit whom the Father will send in my name, will teach you all things and bring to your remembrance all that I have said to you." Only the Spirit can comprehend the things of God, yet God uses human messengers—remembrancers—to impart those things (1 Cor 2:11-13).

An antimony exists when two undeniable yet apparently irreconcilable truths stand side by side. Each one is built on solid evidence, but no one can understand or explain how both can be true simultaneously.[22] The old conundrum between God's sovereignty and human responsibility is an antimony—both statements are perfectly true yet the human mind cannot see how that is so.

The first three chapters have laid a foundation in theology and other disciplines for serving as a remembrancer. The remaining chapters now turn to methodology. Ministers stir memory through effective language, story, delivery, and ceremony.

---

[22]J. I. Packer, *Evangelism and the Sovereignty of God* (Downers Grove, IL: InterVarsity Press, 1961), 18-24.

4

STYLE AS A TOOL FOR STIRRING MEMORY

It is not enough to know what we ought to say;

we must also say it as we ought;

much help is thus afforded toward producing

the right impression of a speech.

ARISTOTLE, *RHETORIC*

The truth must dazzle.

EMILY DICKENSON

If true religion lies much in the affections,

we may infer, that such a way of preaching the word . . .

as has a tendency deeply to affect the hearts of those

who attend . . . is much to be desired.

JONATHAN EDWARDS, *RELIGIOUS AFFECTIONS*

To say that it is possible to persuade

without speaking to the passions,

is but, at best a kind of specious nonsense.

GEORGE CAMPBELL, *PHILOSOPHY OF RHETORIC*

●

An ancient Chinese story describes a powerful king who sees an ox being led to slaughter.[1] Perhaps the ox senses what is about to happen since it trembles like a puppy. Moved with pity, the king orders the handlers to locate a sheep to be used in its place. Later the king is challenged for being stingy—slaughtering a sheep instead of an ox. He defends himself by confessing that he did so because he could see the ox but not the sheep.

This story illustrates how concrete experience stirs the affections and leads to action. It also illustrates the opposite: out of sight, out of mind. For the king, the thought of a sheep being slaughtered was just that—an abstract thought. It evoked no pity.

Remembrancers stir the affections not with actual objects such as oxen and sheep, but with words. We mobilize language and send it into battle against the devil who schemes to make Christians drift from the faith. Vivid language rouses slumbering knowledge, values, and feelings, so that people are re-membered to the great truths of the faith. A bland recitation of truth will be met with a shrug and a yawn, so the old, old story must become "present" once again.

STYLE: HOW IT WORKS

In rhetorical theory the use of language is called *style*, and it is one of the five canons of ancient rhetoric. Style is much more than ornament or embellishment like tinsel adorning the bare branches of a Christmas tree. Rather, it is a tool of persuasion. Style cannot be separated from content because language is the boxcar that carries the freight of meaning. Modern philosopher Richard Weaver brings style and content together in his definition of rhetoric: "truth plus its artful presentation."[2] Francis Bacon's statement is similar: "The duty and office of Rhetoric is to apply Reason to Imagination for the better moving of the will."[3] This chapter treats style as a powerful force that ministers can use as they

---

[1]Recounted in Chaim Perelman and L. Olbrechts-Tyteca, *The New Rhetoric: A Treatise on Argumentation* (Notre Dame, IN: University of Notre Dame Press, 1969), 116.

[2]Richard Weaver, *The Ethics of Rhetoric* (South Bend, IN: Gateway, 1953), 15.

[3]Francis Bacon, *Selected Writings of Francis Bacon*, ed. Hugh C. Dick (New York: Modern Library, 1955), x.

keep watch over souls. Vivid language actualizes what is dormant. It captures attention and compels assent by causing the mind to process information in ways that correspond to actual sensory experience.

My approach to style draws from George Campbell, an eighteenth-century Scottish minister and rhetorician, for the theory of vivid language he calls *vivacity*. Campbell's approach to style is grounded in the neuroscience of the day, what he calls the "operations of the mind": imagination, memory, and direct sensory experience. Similar to Campbell's theory is Perelman and Olbrechts-Tyteca's theory of presence—highlighting in the minds and feelings of the listeners what the persuader wants them to focus on. To use a metaphor from film, presence occurs when the camera zooms in on the subject and leaves the background behind.[4]

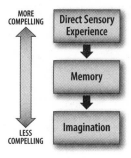

Figure 1. Three operations of the mind

At the top of the hierarchy might be an attack by a dog (direct sensory experience). This event compels involuntary attention and assent because it is emotionally charged and physically experienced. It cannot be denied. No one has to convince you the attack is real and dire. The second level of the hierarchy—memories of the dog attack—are the footprints left behind by direct sensory experience. At times, memory prompts emotional and cognitive responses nearly identical to the actual experience. At other times memory is hazy and distant.

---

[4]George Campbell, *The Philosophy of Rhetoric*, ed. Lloyd Bitzer (Carbondale: Southern Illinois University Press, 1988), 73-81; Perelman and Olbrechts-Tyteca, *The New Rhetoric*, 115-20, 142.

The third level is imagination. If a person has no experience of an attack (and thus no memory of an attack) the speaker must help him or her imagine the experience by using vivid language, one of the primary instruments in the preacher's tool belt to compel attention, arouse emotion, and win assent. Preaching that lacks style (in the rhetorical sense of that word) rarely gains a hearing. Abstract, boring, impersonal, and bland words are like seed that falls on hard soil, quickly snatched by the birds before it penetrates the ground and sprouts.

Figure 2. An example of the three operations of the mind

Ministers rarely use direct sensory experience in their sermons.[5] Conversely, ministers do use memory when preaching to believers because the saints have previously experienced the presence of God. They have tasted and seen that the Lord is good. The preacher reminds folks of that sweet taste and offers it anew. Although believers are prone to forget, by virtue of their union with Christ they can be re-minded of God's love and holiness, re-called to their covenant responsibilities, and re-membered to Christ and his body. Vivid language is vital in that endeavor.

Vivid language is also essential in the third operation: imagination. This is the one ministers employ most commonly. For example, when Jonathan Edwards preached "Sinners in the Hands of An Angry God,"

---

[5]This statement needs to be qualified. While it is true that preachers rarely use direct experience while they are speaking—as when Marc Antony displays the body of Caesar, stabbed and bloody, to turn the crowd against Brutus in *Julius Caesar*—their delivery is a kind of direct experience for the audience. Preaching is embodied communication (see chapter six). Additionally, preaching as reminding works with ceremonies such as the Lord's Supper and baptism—direct sensory experience (see chapter seven).

he could not actually dangle listeners over the pit of hell (direct sensory experience), neither could he stir memory of actual experience, so he used vivid language to spark imagination, and this prompted the people of New England to repent. Warning his people to flee from the wrath to come, Edwards vivified half-believed truths, roused slumbering feelings, and revived dormant faith.

Figure 3. Language and the operations of the mind in Jonathan Edwards's sermon

My emphasis on vivid language, emotion, and imagination warrants a caveat: the use of style is not an end in itself. It is a handmaiden to explanation and persuasion and, for the purposes of this book, to the ministry of reminding. Effective style does not call attention to itself but rather to the content of the discourse, and ultimately to the glory of God. C. S. Lewis's metaphor is apropos—language can be used as a spectacle, causing folks to marvel at its artistry, or it can be a pair of spectacles by which we see something else more clearly.[6] The latter is the approach ministers should aspire to.

To use a different figure, when verbal artistry struts on center stage, the purposes of the discourse are forced to the wings. Aristotle goes so far as to say that "a writer must disguise his art and give the impression of speaking naturally and not artificially. Naturalness is persuasive, artificiality is the contrary."[7] Using yet another figure—a

---

[6]Summarized in Alister McGrath, *C. S. Lewis, A Life: Eccentric Genius, Reluctant Prophet* (Carol Stream, IL: Tyndale, 2013), 287.

[7]Aristotle, *The Rhetoric and Poetics of Aristotle*, trans. W. Rhys Roberts (New York: Modern Library, 1954), 167.

"golden key"—Augustine argues that an eloquent style is necessary at times, but only at times. When not necessary, he says leave it behind: "What use is a golden key, if it cannot unlock what we want to be unlocked, and what is wrong with a wooden [key], if it can, since our sole aim is to open closed doors?"[8] A vivid yet conversational style will open nearly any door.

The florid style of nineteenth-century oratory, what Richard Weaver calls the "spaciousness of old rhetoric,"[9] will not open many doors in most Western cultures today because it calls attention to itself, distracting listeners from the speaker's aim. The eloquence that delighted the crowds at the feet of Daniel Webster and William Jennings Bryan would strike the modern ear as verbose and self-conscious. In the electronic age the "fireside chat" is more effective than the purple prose of the past. Of course, we can point to exceptions. Even in the electronic age, the power of a memorable, metaphorical phrase, such as "I have a dream," still has great impact.[10]

STYLE: HOW TO WORK IT

A whole book could be written on sermonic style (indeed, books have been written[11]), so we must necessarily pick and choose a few techniques that open closed doors. These techniques are best learned from imitation, as is true of much of the art of homiletics, but the term "imitation" does not mean thoughtless mimicking; rather, it means observation of the masters and incorporation of the principles they display into one's own practice.[12]

---

[8] Augustine, *On Christian Teaching*, translated and edited by R. P. H. Green (Oxford: Oxford University Press, 1997), 4.11.

[9] Weaver, *Ethics of Rhetoric*, 164-85.

[10] Kathleen Hall Jamieson, *Eloquence in an Electronic Age: The Transformation of Political Speechmaking* (Oxford: Oxford University Press, 1990), 43-66.

[11] See Jay E. Adams, *Sense Appeal in the Sermons of Charles Haddon Spurgeon*, Studies in Preaching 1 (Nutley, NJ: Presbyterian and Reformed, 1976); Mark Galli and Craig Brian Larson, *Preaching that Connects: Using Journalistic Techniques to Add Impact* (Grand Rapids: Zondervan, 1994); Jolyon P. Mitchell, *Visually Speaking: Radio and the Renaissance of Preaching* (Louisville, KY: Westminster John Knox, 1999).

[12] George A. Kennedy provides a summary of the practice of imitation in *Classical Rhetoric and Its Christian and Secular Tradition from Ancient to Modern Times* (Chapel Hill, NC: University of North Carolina Press, 1980), 116-19. A modern text in the field of homiletics that uses

Use concrete language. If you were preaching on Ephesians 1:6, "We are accepted in the beloved" (KJV), many in the congregation will have heard that verse previously and given mental assent to it, but the comforting truth of the believer's union with Christ may not have stirred their affections for some time. The sidebar "Accepted in the Beloved" demonstrates how concrete language connects the head to the heart.

ACCEPTED IN THE BELOVED

When I was dating my dear wife, Liz Hansen, I traveled on a Greyhound bus from Pittsburgh, Pennsylvania, to Medford, Oregon, to see her. After seventy-five hours on the bus I pulled into the station at one a.m., scruffy and unwashed. Squinting through the bus window, I saw Liz and her mother, who had come to pick me up.

I had never met Mrs. Hansen before, so Liz introduced us: "Mom, this is Jeff. Jeff, this is my mother."

With a broad smile she looked me over and after a few seconds said, "We're so glad you came to visit. Let's go!" We drove to 46 Summit Avenue, and Mrs. Hansen showed me the guest room—fresh sheets, clean towels, and a warm comforter. She made me a snack—leftover chicken and toast—and as we sat at the kitchen table, she handed me keys to the house and the car. She said, "While you're here, our house is your house. Make yourself at home." She smiled again, looked me over again, and seemed satisfied with what she saw.

Why did she do that? Because of my striking good looks? No. Because of my charming personality? No. Because I could pay her handsomely? No!

She lavished grace on me because she had accepted me in the beloved, her beloved baby daughter, Liz. She loved her daughter, and her daughter loved me, and that was good enough for Mrs. Hansen.

---

imitation is Paul Scott Wilson, *Setting Words on Fire: Putting God at the Center of the Sermon* (Nashville: Abingdon, 2008). In his dissertation Geoffrey Stevenson argues that one of the most effective means of teaching homiletics is through imitation: "Learning to Preach: Social Learning Theory and the Development of Christian Preachers" (PhD diss., University of Edinburgh, 2009).

Concrete language is more interesting than abstract language and is more likely to stir emotion because, as in the story of the Chinese king that opens this chapter, the audience can "see" the thing being described. These words have little chance of sparking imagination: "virtue," "facility," "life," "value," "calculation," "dissent," and "idea," but pictures leap into the mind with words like "beggar," "toupee," "teapot," "dragon," "cornfield," "marshmallow," and "dagger." To be sure, preachers need abstract words such as "compassion" and "destruction," but such terms communicate best when joined with concrete language. When "compassion" is coupled with "Mother Teresa," or "destruction" with "lake of fire," the words can reach the heart. Part of the appeal of our most enduring hymns resides in their use of concrete language. Consider the language from just one verse of "Come Thou Fount of Every Blessing": "debtor," "daily," "constrained," "fetter," "bind," "prone," "wander," "seal," and "courts."

Additionally, concrete language is more easily remembered than abstract language because the human mind is a picture gallery, not an encyclopedia. Neuroscientist Alan Baddeley affirms this: "Words that refer to concrete objects . . . are on the whole more easily remembered than abstract words for which imagery is difficult."[13] The ancient orators recognized this fact thousands of years ago. They had great need for memory because they delivered extended speeches—hours in length—without notes. To help them remember the points of their speeches, they developed intricate and inventive methods based on visual imagery. For example, picturing themselves walking on a road that cuts through a wheat field, they might associate point one with that sight. The journey might continue to an inn that they would associate with point two, and so forth.

If you desire listeners to remember the words "soldier" and "ring," then "The soldier dropped the ring" has less staying power than "The soldier lurched to the middle of the bridge and stopped. With a flick

---

[13] Alan Baddeley, *Your Memory: A User's Guide* (New York: Macmillan, 2004), 32.

of the wrist, he tossed the ring into the ravine, squared his shoulders, and marched to the other side."

The key to speaking with concrete language lies in the verbs and nouns. That is where the action of the sentence struts. When verbs and nouns are vague, adding modifiers (adjectives and adverbs) does not dispel the fog. As stylists Strunk and White state, "The adjective hasn't been built that can pull a weak or inaccurate noun out of a tight place."[14] A lean style sparks imagination better than a verbose style. In general, the more briefly something is communicated, the more power it possesses, as when the rays of the sun are focused with a magnifying glass. Take the general words "person" and "moved"—they cannot be rescued by adding "really small person" and "moved tentatively." Try "The toddler wobbled" or "The ballerina limped." After solidifying the verb and noun, you may not need descriptive words, but when used sparingly, they can add even more color: "The mud-caked toddler wobbled cheerfully across the soggy backyard"; "The undaunted ballerina limped painfully to her dressing room."

To develop skill with concrete verbs, listen to sportscasters summarize the day's games: "The Red Sox *embarrassed* the Yankees 10-1." "The Steelers *squeezed by* the Ravens." "The Trailblazers *crushed* the Lakers for their third straight win." "Team x *mauled, thumped, rolled over*, or *walloped* poor old team y." None of the words above are fancy or erudite; all are within an ordinary speaking vocabulary and the comprehension of the listeners, yet the words are concrete.

An example from John Piper demonstrates how a minister might use concrete language in the ministry of reminding. Piper's goal was to rouse listeners' memory regarding Jesus' prediction that he will come again. It will be awesome, like lightning from the east that shines as far as the west (Mt 24:27). Piper himself was reminded of that truth when he saw a lightning storm while flying over Lake Michigan, so he used vivid language to recount his experience and prompt vicarious

---

[14]William Strunk Jr. and E. B. White, *The Elements of Style*, 3rd ed. (New York: Macmillan, 1979), 71.

experience. He approached the point inductively, first forming the scene in the reader's imagination, eventually arriving at his point:

> As I sat there staring out into the total blackness, suddenly the whole sky was brilliant with light. . . . A mammoth white tunnel of light exploded from north to south across the horizon, and again vanished into blackness. Soon the lightning was almost constant and volcanoes of light burst up out of cloud ravines and from behind distant white mountains. I sat there shaking my head almost in unbelief. "O Lord, if these are but the sparks from the sharpening of your sword, what will be the day of your appearing!"[15]

Many listeners have heard the truth that "Jesus is coming back," yet that truth might be Teflon in their hearts. Piper's style makes it Velcro.

Use metaphor. I am using the term "metaphor" not only in its technical sense of a = b (as when we say "he is a clown"), but also in the general sense of any figurative language that compares one thing to another, such as simile and analogy. These comparisons can be quite brief ("The Lord is my shepherd") or as long as a whole chapter of the Bible, such as Ezekiel 16, which we will look at below. Metaphor adds vivacity to discourse. Compare "Written communication is a more effective way to bring about change than what can be accomplished with weapons" to "The pen is mightier than the sword."

As you know, the Bible abounds with metaphor: God is a rock, shield, tower, king, father, and consuming fire. The Word of God is a lamp, sword, seed, bread, water, milk, hammer, and mirror. Jesus is the cornerstone, shepherd, and bridegroom of the church, and the church itself is a bride, army, family, temple, flock, and royal priesthood. This kind of language is more than grace notes on a musical score, delightful but dispensable; it is profound theology expressed in ways that are compatible with the human mind.[16] To be

---

[15]John Piper, *Desiring God: Meditations of a Christian Hedonist* (Portland, OR: Multnomah, 1987), 84.

[16]George Lakoff and Mark Johnson argue that metaphor pervades language because thinking is largely metaphorical. When confronted with abstractions, the human mind craves images,

sure, theology needs literal language for precision and abstract language for breadth, but theology also needs metaphor to capture aspects of reality that are not easily caged. For example, metaphor is one way, a primary way, we understand the covenant: "A shoot shall come out of the stump of Jesse"; "Enter in through the narrow gate"; "No one can serve two masters"; if you forget God, "the heavens over your head shall be bronze, and the earth under you shall be iron"; "I am the potter, you are the clay"; "All flesh is grass"; "Who can endure the day of his coming for he is like a refiner's fire?" Metaphor does not dumb down theology. Rather, it uses language that everyone speaks fluently.

The importance of metaphor to theology is evident when we examine hymns, those poetic distillations of the faith. For example, the pregnant image of the ocean is used three ways in three hymns. The love of Jesus is

> Vast, unmeasured, boundless, free!
> Rolling as a mighty ocean
> In its fullness over me.[17]

Conversely, "sorrows like sea billows roll"[18] across our lives, and sin and despair are like "the sea waves cold."[19]

A good metaphor is "generative"—it gives birth to ideas and emotions not commonly experienced when we use literal language. Like the flaming torch of a Hawaiian dancer, spinning and throwing out sparks, metaphor coruscates. For example, in a narrative sermon about David and Absalom, Haddon Robinson recounts the background that led to Absalom's revolt: Amnon raped Tamar, Absalom's sister, yet David did not punish him. Absalom nursed his hatred and plotted revenge over an extended period of time. In Robinson's sparkling phrase, "He sucked that lemon for three

---

and those images then condition how we conceive of reality. *Metaphors We Live By* (Chicago: University of Chicago Press, 1980), 3-5.

[17]Samuel Trevor Francis, "O the Deep, Deep Love of Jesus," 1875.
[18]Horatio G. Spafford, "It Is Well with My Soul," 1873.
[19]Julia H. Johnston, "Grace Greater than Our Sin," 1910.

years."[20] My students and I have remembered that expression for many years.

MAKING THEOLOGY "PRESENT"

How you make the astounding yet abstract theology of Hebrews 1:2-3—through Jesus God created and upholds the universe—"present" to your congregation? You might try a visual-spatial comparison:

The universe is so immense that the mind cannot grasp it. The sun is 93 million miles away. The North Star is 400 trillion miles away. The star Betelgeuse is 880 quadrillion miles away (that's 880 followed by fifteen zeroes). Knowing that the human mind is a picture gallery, not an abacus, one of my students made the abstract vivid by using a visual analogy to help us understand and feel the awe-inspiring theology of Hebrews 1. Holding a tennis ball to represent the sun (2.7 inches in diameter) and the edge of a dime to proportionally represent the earth (0.02 inches), he stepped off twenty-four feet to demonstrate the distance between the sun and the earth.

The classroom was far too small to demonstrate longer distances, so he continued with a verbal analogy to explain the distance to Alpha Centauri, the nearest star: the tennis ball would be in Boston and Alpha Centauri would be in Memphis. The simple visual analogy reached our hearts to remind us of our great God who created and upholds the universe.

Let's say the preacher is speaking from Luke 10:25-37, the Good Samaritan, and her central idea is that "God calls Christians to love their neighbors." That idea has been pulled from the closet so often that it is threadbare, but simile can help: "God calls Christians to love their neighbors, *as* Mother Teresa loved the people of her neighborhood." If the congregation has direct experience of Mother Teresa (unlikely) or secondhand experience of Mother Teresa through books

---

[20]Haddon W. Robinson, "The Broken Heart of David Jessison" (Portland, OR: Multnomah Bible College, 1994), VHS.

or videos (likely) then the bald idea gains some traction in the listeners' hearts. The use of style would be even more powerful by extending the metaphor with a story of Mother Teresa: "God calls Christians to love their neighbors as Mother Teresa did. . . . Let me tell you about a trip I took to India where I actually met Mother Teresa. I was walking through a terrible neighborhood when I saw a group of nuns. . . . They were feeding the poor, their neighbors . . ."

Even better than an example about Mother Teresa would be an example from the listeners' field of experience, perhaps Deacon Smith, whom they all know and love: "God calls Christians to love like Deacon Smith. When I first moved to this area eight years ago, I didn't know Deacon Smith and he didn't know me, but he showed up on my front porch, helped me move furniture, and . . ." When the preacher taps into the congregation's experience, affect is roused and attention is focused. Metaphor helps the minister awaken hibernating truth.

The sentence "Give your very best to your Lord" might sound like Charlie Brown's teacher droning at the front of the class. Perhaps Spurgeon sensed that, so he reasoned with analogy to convey the idea, saving the abstract statement until the end. He says that if you were giving a present to a prince, "you would not find Him a lame horse to ride upon; you would not offer Him a book out of which leaves had been torn, nor carry Him a timepiece whose wheels were broken. No, the best of the best you would give to one whom you honored and loved. Give your very best to your Lord."[21] Lame horses and broken timepieces capture attention, heighten comprehension, and touch the affections in ways more prosaic language does not.

Ezekiel 16 is one of the Bible's most powerful instances of reminding, and not surprisingly, it uses an extended analogy. The Lord reminds idol-worshiping Jerusalem that they were like an infant "cast out on the open field . . . wallowing in [their] blood." God took pity and said, "Live!" The infant grew into a beautiful young woman, and the Lord made a covenant with her so that she became "mine!" Adorned with gold and

---

[21]Charles Spurgeon, "An All-Round Ministry," in Steve Miller, *C. H. Spurgeon on Spiritual Leadership* (Chicago: Moody Press, 2003), 72.

silver, dressed in linen and silk, honored with a crown and chain, she grew "exceedingly beautiful and advanced to royalty," only to turn those adornments into instruments of whoring that she lavished on any passerby. The Lord says, through the prophet, "You did not remember the days of your youth, when you were naked and bare, wallowing in your blood. . . . [So] I have returned your deeds upon your head."

The very nations she claimed as lovers would strip her of her jewels to leave her naked and bare so she would learn to play the whore no longer. But even as she baked in the oven of discipline, the Lord said, "I will remember my covenant with you in the days of your youth, and I will establish for you an everlasting covenant . . . that you may remember and be confounded and never open your mouth again because of your shame, when I atone for you for all that you have done."

That is what remembrancers do. With courage they remind people when they trample the covenant, and with grace they bind up the wounds memory can inflict.

Use repetition and rhythm. Oral style is not written style. Complex syntactic constructions and subordinate clauses, crafted and polished in the study, work well when communicating for the eye because written communication proceeds at the receiver's rate. An individual can read as slowly or as quickly as desired—rereading, skipping, underlining, or skimming—but oral communication proceeds at the sender's rate. To carry the listeners forward in the ephemeral flow of words, effective oral style uses repetition, restatement, redundancy, and review, keeping close to the center of attention the point being made. Furthermore, oral style is conscious of aurality—what words sound like—so that parallelism, rhythm, refrain, and other techniques deriving from the "musicality" of speech contribute to a style that stirs the heart.

Repetition aids the recall of knowledge. Knowledge degrades like uranium but repetition refreshes it. As we saw in chapter two, the brain needs repetition to create neural pathways that lead to changed thought and behavior. This principle operates in Isaiah 28 where the author prescribes repetition by using repetition—"Precept upon precept, precept upon precept, line upon line, line upon line, here a little, there a little" (Is 28:10). Similarly, in Deuteronomy 6:4-9 Moses commands that the Shema ("Hear, O Israel . . .") be repeated with multiple channels and at multiple times of the day. Israelites are to remind themselves when walking, going to bed, and awakening that the Lord is One. God's people are to write the reminder on the doorposts and on the gates. The scientific basis of learning may not have been known in that day, but the power of repetition was. Writing in an entirely different context—piano pedagogy—Andrea McAlister observes:

> The ways in which we learn and form memories haven't changed over the years. We still need information to be presented in manageable quantities and consistently duplicated in order for it to be stored in long-term memory. What has changed, however, is the amount of stimuli with which we are presented daily. If information is only attended to once or twice before the next stimuli invades our attention, those long-term memories are much more difficult to produce.[22]

These observations from ancient Israel and modern pedagogy remind us that for knowledge and skills to be ingrained in the human mind there must be repetition, so ministers patiently instruct and remind in order to keep the faith glowing. In a sense, much of the pastor's work is catechesis. The same Greek root occurs in both *catechesis* and *echo*, suggesting that teaching must be stated and then stated again so that faith will reverberate through the generations.

Repetition and rhythm aid the stirring of emotion. One of the most stirring musical performances I have experienced was an a capella rendition of "A Mighty Fortress Is Our God" by Steve Green. Modulating up a key on each of the four verses, he ended with a soaring climax to God's glory. Green performed this hymn before an audience of one hundred faculty, staff, and donors at the seminary where I teach. Many of us already knew the words of the hymn; in fact, as he was singing he went blank for an instant and asked us what the next lyrics

---

[22]Andrea McAlister, "Technology and the Learning Process," *Clavier Companion* (March/April 2015): 21.

were. More than thirty people answered as one. So the power of the performance did not reside in the newness of the ideas expressed, but in the stirring of old ideas, deeply treasured, expressed through musical poetry—melody, rhythm, rhyme, modulation, and dynamics.

Observing the power of music, Plato said poets and singers had more influence in a state than lawmakers: "Musical training is a more potent instrument than any other, because rhythm and harmony find their way into the inward places of the soul."[23] I believe it is possible to capture some of the effects of music in our sermons. Repetition, rhythm, and parallelism are arrows of eloquence that pierce the heart.

The Bible models repetition and rhythm. These qualities contribute to some of its most beautiful and best-loved passages, such as Ruth's speech to Naomi: "Where you go I will go, and where you lodge I will lodge. Your people shall be my people, and your God my God. Where you die I will die, and there will I be buried" (Ruth 1:16-17). Notice how 1 Corinthians 13:7 uses only seven different words in a sentence of thirteen words (eight words are repeated): "Love bears all things, believes all things, hopes all things, endures all things." In the soaring crescendo of Romans 8, Paul may achieve the highest level of eloquence in all of his writings:

> Who shall separate us from the love of Christ? Shall tribulation, or distress, or persecution, or famine, or nakedness, or danger, or sword? . . . No, in all these things we are more than conquerors through him who loved us. For I am sure that neither death nor life, nor angels nor rulers, nor things present nor things to come, nor powers, nor height nor depth, nor anything else in all creation, will be able to separate us from the love of God in Christ Jesus our Lord. (Rom 8:35-39)

Eloquence soars on the wings of repetition and rhythm. This passage from one of my own sermons concerning the hollowness of the American dream uses repetition and rhythm for persuasion and memory:

---

[23]Plato, *The Republic*, 3.398-403, theoryofmusic.wordpress.com/2008/04/music-in-platos -republic.

You work hard in high school so you can get into a dream college, then you study hard in college so you can get a dream job; you work overtime at your dream job so you can drive a dream car, and that helps you attract a dream spouse; you have a dream wedding, move into a dream house, and have 1.7 dream kids; then you save money to take a dream vacation to get away from the dream kids; then you plug away to build up a dream 401(k) so you can take a dream retirement.

Then you die.

And you have a dream funeral with a dream casket that is placed in a dream hole in the ground.

Isn't there something better than the American dream?

Effective style does not call attention to itself like a stained glass window; rather, it is a pane of clear glass that shows us something beyond itself. But for the most intense moments of the sermon—often the conclusion, or what the ancient rhetoricians called the "peroration"—language that transcends the style of everyday conversation can open and even pierce the heart.

Such language was on display in a eulogy Ted Kennedy gave for his brother Robert: "My brother need not be idealized, or enlarged in death beyond what he was in life; to be remembered simply as a good and decent man, who saw wrong and tried to right it, saw suffering and tried to heal it, saw war and tried to stop it."[24] In technical terms, Kennedy uses a device called "symploce," which repeats the beginning and end of each phrase but alters the middle. "He *saw* wrong and tried to stop *it*, *saw* suffering and tried to heal *it*, *saw* war and tried to stop *it*." The heightened rhetorical effect takes place by means of grammatical structure, not vocabulary. All the italicized words are one syllable and well within the speaking vocabulary of every listener.[25]

---

[24]Edward M. Kennedy, "Address at the Public Memorial Service for Robert F. Kennedy," American Rhetoric Top 100 Speeches, delivered June 8, 1968, www.americanrhetoric.com/speeches/ekennedytributetorfk.html.

[25]Cornelius Plantinga Jr., *Reading for Preaching: The Preacher in Conversation with Storytellers, Biographers, Poets, and Journalists* (Grand Rapids: Eerdmans, 2013), 51-52.

TWO STIRRING PERORATIONS

To bring together the strands of this chapter on style, read aloud the "perorations" from two powerful sermons. I was present for both of these memorable events.

"Building on the Right Foundation," by Dr. Tony Evans

This sermon by Tony Evans is an exposition of the parable of the two builders (Mt 7:24-27). Dr. Evans reminded his listeners that obeying Christ's Word forms a solid foundation for a life that can withstand the storms of adversity. The illustration of one house built on sand and the other built on rock uses all the techniques discussed in this chapter: concrete verbs and nouns, metaphor, repetition, and rhythm. In addition, it also uses techniques we will discuss in coming chapters—story and delivery. Use your imagination to see Tony's gestures as he mimes striking the punching bag, and hear Tony's voice as the punching bag bounces from side to side ("boom, boom, boom") before standing upright again ("bing!").

> When I was growing up my father purchased for me a blue boxing bag. When you hit it—"bam!"—it would ricochet off the floor—"boom, boom, boom"—and bounce back—"bing!" Punch it hard—"bam!" and what did it do? "Boom, boom, boom, bing!" I remember getting mad one time and kicking it—"bam, boom, boom, boom, boom, boom . . . bing!" It just kept coming back. Do you know why? Because at the bottom of the bag was a weight. The foundation was heavier than the rest of the bag. And so the weight at the bottom determined where the bag finally wound up, no matter what you did to it.
>
> I wish I could tell you that life had no difficulties waiting for you. But the Bible doesn't tell us that. But when the storms of life go "bam!" you will come back. When Satan goes "whap!" you will come back. When all hell breaks loose—"bam, bam, bam!"—you're going to bounce around and come back—"boom, boom, boom, bing!" Because after the hurricane is over, the man who builds his house on the rock will stand.[a]

"Sermon from Job," by Dr. Bryan Carter

In Dr. Bryan Carter's "Sermon from Job," Carter preached for almost forty minutes with great fervor. But in the peroration he pulled out all the stops to remind his audience of pastors that God is still good, even when they walk through the valley. As you read aloud, learn by imitation, remembering that imitation is not slavish copying but the incorporation of principles into your own style.

> In November of 2002 Pastor E. K. Bailey was diagnosed with cancer. He went away for treatment, which took two to three months—chemotherapy and radiation. He finally came back to the church, and one of his first sermons was entitled "God Is Still Good." He stood with a walker, and he had to drink a lot of water because of the dryness caused by the radiation, but the message was this, "God Is Still Good."

> And I imagine that if you ask Job about God's goodness, Job would say in chapter forty-two "God is still good." That's different than "God is good." "God is good," is something you learn in a lecture class, but "God is still good," is something you learn in the lab. When you say that "God is still good," it means you've been through some difficulty to find out that God is still good. It means you tried him for yourself.

> Weeping may endure for a night, but joy comes in the morning. God is still good. You meant it for evil, but God meant it for good for the saving of many lives. God is still good. We know that he causes all things to work together for the good of those that love him. God is still good. Though they slay me, yet will I trust him. God is still good. Nailed hands. God is still good. Nailed feet. God is still good. A crown of thorns. God is still good. A pierced side. God is still good. He hung his head and died. God is still good. A dead body. God is still good. All day Friday. God is still good. All day Saturday. God is still good. All night Saturday night. God is still good. But early, Sunday morning he got up with all power in his hand. God is still good. God is still good. Yes![b]

[a]Tony Evans, "Building on the Right Foundation," PreachingToday, www.preaching today.com/sermons/outlines/2010/july/buildingontherightfoundation.html, accessed April 3, 2017.

[b]Bryan Carter, "Sermon from Job" (sermon, E. K. Bailey Conference on Expository Preaching, Dallas, TX, July 2013).

Style is a means of persuasion, or, for the interests of this book, it is a trumpet to awaken hibernating faith. In the next chapter we build on the theory of style to look at story—one of the most effectual modes of discourse ever discovered for re-membering the covenant community to its first love.

5

STORY AS A TOOL
FOR STIRRING MEMORY

Time didn't start this emphasis on stories about people; the Bible did.

HENRY LUCE, FOUNDER OF *TIME* MAGAZINE

I love to tell the story; for those who know it best
Seem hungering and thirsting to hear it like the rest.

KATHERINE HANKEY

He said nothing to them without a parable.

MATTHEW 13:34

●

DR. OLIVER SACKS HAS MADE A couple of appearances in this book. He is the neurologist who worked with Jimmie and whose writings provided the basis for the movie *Awakenings*. Another Sacks story recounts the transformation of Virgil, who went blind as a toddler.[1] As an adult he agrees to groundbreaking cataract surgery in the chance that it might restore his sight. After the surgery, as the doctor gently removes the bandages, he asks, "What do you see; what do you see?"

---

[1] The print version is in Oliver Sacks, *An Anthropologist on Mars: Seven Paradoxical Tales* (New York: Alfred A. Knopf, 1995). The film version is *At First Sight*, directed by Irwin Winkler (Hollywood, CA: Metro-Goldwyn-Mayer, 1998).

Virgil doesn't know what he sees. All is a blur and kaleidoscope. Distraught, he replies, "I don't know . . . something's wrong. This can't be seeing." He has no vocabulary for shapes and colors, and he has no memories to correlate this experience with others. Virgil's sister confronts the doctor in the hallway, who calms her by saying, "Believe me, he can see you. He just doesn't understand what he sees."

Virgil gradually develops enough visual literacy to leave the hospital, but his adventure is just beginning. A shadow on the sidewalk shocks him. An object brought close to his eyes appears to grow larger and he cringes. The changing shape of a dog as it curls, stretches, or walks bewilders him.

The change from sequential to holistic processing of experience can overwhelm the newly sighted. Touch and hearing are sequential, but sight is holistic, as when we "read" facial expression: one glimpse reveals all. As a blind person Virgil recognized objects and sounds only as he experienced them in time, first touching one part of an object and then another, so as a sighted person Virgil could not tell the difference between a cat and a dog by using only vision. He had to touch them while viewing them, associating what he saw with what he felt. Even then Virgil had to regularly repeat the process of stroking and staring at whiskers, ears, tails, and feet before he was ready to pronounce "cat!" or "dog!" Virgil's wife observed, "You'd think once was enough," but Sacks comments, "The new ideas, the visual recognitions, kept slipping from his mind."[2]

It's the same with us. Virgil's experience of learning to see is like the believer's experience of faith. We are learning to correlate the sequential episodes of our lives with a holistic, God's-eye view of reality. The promotion (or demotion) we receive at work, the encouraging (or discouraging) report from the doctor, and the acceptance (or rejection) of our proposal are pieces of the grand plan God has authored for each of us, a plan in which he works all things together for the good of those who love him. Standing outside of time, he sees all at a glance, but dwelling

---

[2]Sacks, *Anthropologist on Mars*, 122.

in time we see through a glass darkly, and the sequence of our lives can seem formless and void. Thus we need the ministry of remembrancers who name reality with theological accuracy and pastoral patience. One of the best ways to do this is with story.

STORY: HOW IT WORKS

Narrative is present in every age, in every place, among every society. No culture exists without it. As Alasdair MacIntyre has stated, the human being is "essentially a story-telling animal."[3] This may be because we experience reality in a narrative-like way—as characters in a setting who go through one event after another, even if those events feel more like chronicle than story.[4] Chronicle is a record of unrelated events—"the king died and then the queen died"—but story depicts a unified and complete action with causes and consequences—"the king died and then the queen died of grief." Choosing from an infinite array of details, the storyteller selects and arranges just a few to provide a perspective on why things happen as they do. In Roderick Hart's phrase, stories are "depropositionalized argument" that use both rational and intuitive ways of knowing.[5]

Argument presented in the beguiling form of story utilizes one of the most powerful modes of communication we possess. Four characteristics of story help explain its power and why those who stir memory should keep it close at hand.

Imagination and emotion. Every experienced preacher knows that story rivets attention and increases retention. Who has not experienced the magic of words like these: "That reminds me of the time when I was in high school. My friends and I went spelunking in a dark, dripping cave in the hills of western Pennsylvania." Heads rise, eyes focus, and fidgets cease as neurons in the centers of the brain associated with sensory experience, emotion, and cognition fire together.

---

[3] Alasdair MacIntyre, *After Virtue: A Study in Moral Theory*, 3rd ed. (Notre Dame, IN: University of Notre Dame Press, 2007), 216.

[4] Stephen Crites, "The Narrative Quality of Experience," *Journal of the American Academy of Religion* 39, no. 3 (1971): 291-311.

[5] Roderick Hart, *Modern Rhetorical Criticism* (Glenview, IL: Scott Foresman, 1990), 133.

The brain functions more holistically when hearing a story than when hearing, "The third reason God has pronounced blessing on the faithful can be found in verse four."

This is not to say that propositions have no place in preaching.[6] In fact, biblical preaching is necessarily propositional because it is the declaration of good news—an announcement of a historical fact with its world-changing implications—but concepts need images for actualization to occur. The concept of "worldview" is aptly named because our vision of reality includes images as well as ideas. As Henry David Thoreau said, "A fact stated barely is dry. It must be the vehicle of some humanity in order to interest us. It is like giving a man a stone when he asks you for bread."[7]

The previous chapter explored how vivid language rouses imagination and emotion, so there is no need to call that witness to the stand again except to remind us that details captivate. Concrete verbs and nouns are the stuff of effective storytelling. They increase attention, spark imagination, rouse emotion, and enhance retention.

One way story works this magic is through form—the arousing and fulfilling of desire.[8] Works of literature produce a sense of disequilibrium and then resolution, just as a musical chord moves from unresolved to resolved, giving the listener a feeling of satisfaction. In the same way, and with the same effect, the plot of a story moves from conflict to resolution. Once a listener steps onto the path with "once upon a time," she or he desires to walk it to the end with "happily ever after." Perhaps this is why Aristotle called plot the "soul" of story.[9]

---

[6]Two sources that defend the necessity of propositions in preaching, even while appreciating the benefits of narrative, are Bryan Chapell, *Using Illustrations to Preach with Power*, rev. ed. (Wheaton, IL: Crossway, 2005), 177-92; and James W. Thompson, *Preaching Like Paul: Homiletical Wisdom for Today* (Louisville, KY: Westminster John Knox, 2001), 1-19.

[7]Quoted in Warren W. Wiersbe, *Preaching and Teaching With Imagination: The Quest for Biblical Ministry* (Wheaton, IL: Victor, 1994), 56.

[8]The term "form" is used in various ways by artists, literary critics, and rhetoricians. My use comes from twentieth-century philosopher and rhetorician Kenneth Burke, who described it as a psychological phenomenon—the arousing and fulfilling of desire. Kenneth Burke, *Counter-Statement* (Berkeley, CA: University of California Press, 1968), 29-44, 123-49; *A Rhetoric of Motives* (Berkeley, CA: University of California Press, 1969), 65-77.

[9]Aristotle, *The Rhetoric*, trans. W. Rhys Roberts (New York: Modern Library, 1954), 1450a.

Without conflict and resolution, no story exists, just as no person exists without a soul. Form helps explain why stories work—how they engage imagination and emotion to waken somnambulant beliefs.

In addition to philosophers, neuroscientists have also described the dynamics of story. Their terminology is different, but they arrive at a similar conclusion—namely, that story is a whole-brain mode of communication that engages the centers of the brain allocated to imagination and emotion as well as cognition. Neuroscientist Ernest Rossi states, "Although stories may appear imprecise and unscientific, they serve as powerful tools for the work of neural network integration at a high level."[10] The networks fire together as listeners empathize with characters, experience catharsis, and pause for self-reflection. When a story is over, its effects continue to simmer.

Clarification by articulation. Story not only rouses emotion, it also clarifies knowledge. Before we articulate our experience—that is, before we tell our story—it is not "present." An unspoken thought or experience is often murky, opaque, or inchoate. Articulating experience with words seals the experience in the sense that it identifies and authenticates it, as when a wax seal is placed on a letter.

The language we use reflects our worldview, and it also shapes it, because words are a "terministic screen" that allows some grains of reality to sift into the heart but also prevents other grains from falling through.[11] What vocabulary do we use to describe the succession of sights and sounds, experiences and enterprises called *life*? That is, what stories do we tell? Is life a tale told by an idiot, full of sound and fury, signifying nothing? Or is it a pilgrimage from the City of Destruction to the Celestial City with each step overseen by the Lord, the governor of the country, who does all things well? Are man and

---

[10]Ernest Rossi, *The Psychobiology of Mind-Body Healing* (New York: Norton, 1986), in Richard H. Cox, *Rewiring Your Preaching: How the Brain Processes Sermons* (Downers Grove, IL: InterVarsity Press, 2012), 41.

[11]Kenneth Burke, *Language as Symbolic Action: Essays on Life, Literature, and Method* (Berkeley: University of California Press, 1966), 44-62. Burke states, "Even if any given terminology is a reflection of reality, by its very nature as a terminology it must be a selection of reality; and to this extent it must function also as a deflection of reality," 45.

woman simply bipeds who have developed opposable thumbs, or are they crowned with glory and honor, made just a little lower than the angels? Indeed, is the entire creation the result of the random collocation of atoms, or is it an artist's masterpiece, marred by the fall but still displaying the marks of genius? The stories we tell shape how we view reality. They are a grammar of thought.

I saw this at work at church on Easter Sunday in 2016. A young couple shared their stories of coming to faith over a period of ten years. During the first years they could not name their experience but were aware only of a kaleidoscopic swirl of doubts, questions, and feelings of purposelessness. Then they started attending church and learned a vocabulary from the stories they heard. They learned that "the heart is restless until it rests in God," and that without God we are like "sheep with a shepherd." Building on that vocabulary, they learned another word: *gospel.* With the tone of doxology, the young couple shared their stories, and the rest of the covenant community relived their own stories. In doing so, the community was re-membered to the gospel of God.

Clarification by articulation can occur even when the story is fiction. For example, the long-lasting interest in The Chronicles of Narnia lies in part in the human intuition that our own stories are part of a larger, grander metanarrative. C. S. Lewis realized that the intersection of our micronarratives with God's macronarrative can all be seen more clearly when "dipped in a story."[12] Through myth, an author enables us to peer around a curtain to see the drama of redemption taking place and how we can find our roles that play.

Our Lord knew the power of fiction to clarify. Rather than simply tossing his listeners a bone of definition when discussing the concept of "neighbor," he served a three-course meal in the parable of the good Samaritan. Rather than handing his followers a freeze-dried principle stating that disciples ought to pray and not lose heart, he served a tasty dish in the parable of the persistent widow. Story

---

[12]Quoted in Alistair McGrath, *C. S. Lewis, A Life: Eccentric Genius, Reluctant Prophet* (Carol Stream, IL: Tyndale, 2014), 279.

clarifies abstract concepts, engages emotion and intuition, and lodges in long-term memory.

Identification and community. Story enfolds listeners into the thoughts, feelings, and experiences of the characters. This is called *identification*. My headache is not your headache, but when I talk about my headache, you draw on your own past experience to imagine what the headache feels like. In other words, you identify and re-member. Story subtly tells listeners that they are part of a community. John Steinbeck said it this way: "No story has power, nor will it last unless we feel in ourselves that it is true and true of us. . . . If the story is not about the hearer, he won't listen."[13]

Biblical narrators leverage the power of identification when they recite the stories of kings and commoners, saints and sinners. They select and arrange materials to evoke responses. That's what Paul implies as he warns the Corinthians by means of a handful of stories from the exodus: "These things took place as examples for us. These things [stories] . . . were written down for our instruction" (1 Cor 10: 6, 11). Empathy for heroes, antipathy for villains, encour-agement to obey God, and warning for the errant occur through the amazing but subtle power of story.

Not only does identification have the potential to rebuke and en-courage, it also builds community, and the species of story that builds community best is testimony. Walls fall, facades crumble, and masks are discarded when someone opens his or her heart with a personal story. Self-disclosure tends to produce a reciprocal response from the hearers as trust increases.[14] One disclosure prompts another. This re-ciprocal function of testimony is especially prevalent when the speaker is an authority such as a pastor sharing from the pulpit. When pastors pull down the blackout curtains to talk about their own experience of following Christ, light illuminates the neighborhood and a culture of transparency forms in the church. Of course, self-disclosure entails

---

[13]John Steinbeck, *East of Eden* (New York: Penguin, 2002), 266-68.
[14]Julia T. Wood, *Interpersonal Communication: Everyday Encounters*, 3rd ed. (Belmont, CA: Wadsworth, 2002), 269-71.

risks as well as rewards so it's best to proceed slowly and with wisdom, but all in all, the benefits are worth the risks.[15]

Testimony shows believers that they are part of the covenant community, a valuable reminder for members of individualistic cultures. We see that our patch of fabric comes from a great bolt of the community's narrative and ultimately from God's great metanarrative of redeeming the world in Christ.

Story helps form community, and community helps us remember or relearn our own stories. We do not usually recollect in isolation; rather, we remember as we share stories with our family and faith family. Community becomes a greenhouse to nurture our sense of self, society, and God.

Indirection. This is a subtle quality that helps explain how story works. When story presents a depropositionalized interpretation of reality, argument walks through the back door of consciousness. The mode of discourse begins, "You are wrong; let me prove it to you" causes listeners to take a defensive stance because a fight is coming. Conversely, "Once upon a time," or "And it came to pass," or "Let me tell you about the time . . ." causes listeners to pull up an armchair. Just ask Nathan and David, who could offer a graduate seminar in the beguiling and indirect power of story. David thought he was strolling through the neighborhood with Nathan, but then he discovered that Nathan had led him to a minefield. Memory exploded and prompted repentance. If Nathan had used direct confrontation, memory might have exploded, but it might have also calcified David's heart (2 Sam 12:1-15).

The "indirect function" of story may seem to be at odds with the ministry of reminding because that ministry is usually done with directness and urgency, as with Moses' repeated exhortations in Deuteronomy—for example: "Remember and do not forget how you provoked the Lord your God" (Deut 9:7), and "You shall remember that you were a slave in the land of Egypt" (Deut 15:15). How then does

---

[15]See Jeffrey D. Arthurs and Andrew Gurevich, "Theological and Rhetorical Perspectives on Self-Disclosure in Preaching," *Bibliotheca Sacra* 157 (April-June 2000): 215-26.

an indirect mode of communication—story—remind? It does so by causing listeners to employ multiple neural networks to empathize and reflect. As we listen to a story, we draw on our own past experiences to put ourselves in the place of the characters. That's why indirection works when the audience is hostile (David and Nathan illustrate this as well). Such an audience can be re-membered to the Lord's will when truth approaches from an oblique angle. As Emily Dickinson advised, "Tell all the truth but tell it slant."[16] Indirect story also can be combined with direct exhortation, just as Nathan followed his parable with the pronouncement "You are the man!" Story garners the benefits described above—emotion and identification—and exhortation adds clarity and urgency.

No one explored the subtle power of indirection with more insight than Fred Craddock, one of the leading homileticans of the twentieth century. In *Overhearing the Gospel* Craddock says that preachers must "awaken," "stir up," "elicit," and "evoke" memories that have "grown fuzzy." Story serves like a "midwife who helps to bring forth" that which is hidden into the light of day.[17]

STORY: HOW TO WORK IT

Many techniques can be used to stir memory with the amazing power of story. I have chosen the following not as a complete catalogue and final word on the subject, but as a way to affirm and enhance what most ministers currently do.

Retell Bible stories. If you feel you need permission to "merely" retell biblical stories, I give you permission. Even more, I *exhort* you to retell the old, old stories. Don't shrink back because you might seem unoriginal. That fear has no place in the motives of heralds because their job is to accurately transmit the message already delivered. Furthermore, don't be afraid of boring the covenant community. That fear does not take into account the fact that believers need to be reminded of their

---

[16]Emily Dickinson, "Tell All the Truth but Tell It Slant," *The Poems of Emily Dickinson: Reading Edition*, ed. Ralph W. Franklin (Cambridge, MA: Harvard University Press: 1951).
[17]Fred B. Craddock, *Overhearing the Gospel*, rev. and exp. (St. Louis: Chalice, 2002), 77.

great God. Furthermore, the fear does not acknowledge the delight believers have in hearing again the history of their faith and the tales of their ancestors who walked with God. As stated earlier, we are like the hobbits who "liked to have books filled with things that they already knew, set out fair and square with no contradictions."[18]

The form of story rouses and fulfills expectations even when the information of the story is already known. Just as moviegoers enjoy watching Luke Skywalker blow up the Death Star two, three, four, or eleven times, so believers enjoy hearing again about Abraham and Isaac, David and Goliath, Mary and Martha, and Jesus raising Lazarus. The enjoyment lies not in suspense because the audience knows how the story turns out. Rather, the enjoyment lies in form and the affirmation of truth. Certainty delights. C. S. Lewis' analogy illustrates this: hikers leave the road to take a shortcut through the forest, but they find themselves lost. The sun sinks and the forest grows black. The hikers stumble in the undergrowth and slog through the dew. But suddenly they burst from the forest and feel again the solid pavement underfoot. How delightful! The stars shine again and the lights of the inn are directly before them.[19]

So don't be afraid to "merely" retell the stories of the Bible. Of course, we must immediately qualify this point. Simply retelling Bible stories does not guarantee effective reminding. Stories can bore or confuse, just as three points and a poem can. The story must be told with vivid language, effective delivery (the subject of the next chapter), and identification. To prompt identification, preachers as reminders begin with themselves. They take the necessary time in sermon preparation to identify with the characters and feel the form of the plot. Once that work is done, effective language and delivery release the magic of story for the listeners.[20] A well-worn idea such as "God is sovereign" comes alive through the story of Job. "God redeems

---

[18]J. R. R. Tolkien, *The Fellowship of the Ring* (New York: Ballantine Books, 1954), 9.

[19]C. S. Lewis, *Reflections on the Psalms* (London: Geoffrey Bles, 1958), 55.

[20]For practical help in crafting narrative sermons, see Jeffrey D. Arthurs, *Preaching With Variety: How to Recreate the Dynamics of the Text* (Grand Rapids: Kregel, 2007), 62-101.

vulnerable foreigners" takes wings with the story of Ruth. "Sinners try to hide their sin when they feel guilty" is personified, focused, emphasized, and vivified with the stories of kings Saul and David. Most believers know and believe those well-worn truths, but actualization through story makes them efficacious.

Ministers may feel the need for "permission" especially at Christmas and Easter. They may feel, "Here we go again. What in the world am I going to say that is fresh?" Banish that fear. It's true that ministers are called to teach new things and prove disputed things, but they are also called to tell the old, old stories of incarnation and resurrection. Just use effective language and delivery, as well as the other techniques we'll discuss ahead, to tell the story well. As the hymn says, even those who know the story best "seem hungering and thirsting to hear it like the rest." Timothy Tennent, president of Asbury Seminary, preached one of the best Christmas sermons I have ever heard. His big idea was simple but well-worded: "Christmas is a riches-to-rags story."[21] All of the faith family knew that truth, but it was heartening to hear it again.

Similarly, Pastor Bobby Warrenburg reminded the members of the church where I worship that Easter did not originate with the sharing of good advice but with the announcing of good news.[22] Warrenburg pointed out that the primary emotion associated with the Gospel accounts of the resurrection was fear, but for us the dominant emotion might be sentimentality or predictability. So he offered "smelling salts for the heart" by "resurrecting Easter" from layers of familiarity. With conviction and joy he announced the good news. He did this by describing the story with imagination and verve, especially the reactions of the witnesses—astonishment, confusion, and fear. The resurrection of Christ "blew their minds" and they were never the same afterwards.

Use dramatization. Dramatization does not mean the staging of a play (although that's another possibility for using narrative). Rather,

---

[21]Timothy Tennent, "Riches to Rags" (sermon, North Shore Community Baptist Church, Beverly Farms, MA, December 2005).

[22]Robert Warrenburg, "Resurrecting Easter" (sermon, North Shore Community Baptist Church, Beverly Farms, MA, March 27, 2016).

it means *showing* the truth, making it come alive by depicting it as a scene in a play. The Roman rhetorician Cicero included what I am calling dramatization in a larger discussion of how to center the audience's attention and rouse pathos. He called the technique *evidentia*—visualizing a scene and involving oneself personally in the subject. Cicero states, "A great impression is made [on the audience] by . . . [an] almost visual presentation of events as if practically going on."[23] This technique serves nearly any rhetorical aim and is especially useful for stirring memory.

"THE SHEEP AND THE GOATS," BY DR. HADDON ROBINSON

Haddon Robinson used dramatization when he preached from Matthew 25 in a seminary chapel, stating, "Whatever you did for the least of these, you did for me."[a] All the students knew that verse, and I imagine some of them had even preached it. So Robinson's job was not to teach a new truth but to vivify an old one.

To accomplish that he transported the seminary audience to the throne room of heaven to stand with him in the judgment of the nations. Robinson capitalized on the power of indirection in two ways: first, through identification. He made himself the main character receiving judgment. The seminary audience was not on trial—or were they? I feel sure that as they overhead the Lord's comments to Robinson, they identified with him and wondered what the Lord would say to them.

Second, he used irony and humor. He described his greatest accomplishments only to see the Lord brush them aside. The students laughed aloud, but as Mark Twain observed, "When mouths are opened in laughter, an author can slip in the pill of truth." They probably concluded that their own mighty accomplishments would also sound trite on the final day.

Notice how Robinson tells the seminary audience what they already know—that serving the "least of these" is equivalent to serving Jesus. He

---

[23]Cicero, *On the Orator*, trans. H. Rackam, ed. Jeffrey Henderson (Cambridge, MA: Harvard University Press, 1942), 161.

could have simply stated that truth, but instead he used dramatization to help them see the scene and identify with himself.

Since it's the judgment of the nations, I imagine I'll be there. I'll be standing before the King and he'll say, "Robinson, did you bring your datebook? Look up October 27, 28, 29, 1983."

"Oh yes, Lord. That's when I was made president of the Evangelical Theological Society. We had a big meeting down in Dallas. I wrote a paper: 'The Relationship of Hermeneutics to Homiletics.'"

And the King will say, "Well, I don't know anything about that. I don't go to many of those meetings. No, what I had in mind happened before you went to Dallas. There was a married couple on your campus. I allowed them to have a twenty-five day check in a thirty-one day month. Bonnie told you about them. And you folks put some money in an envelope and put it in their box. Remember that?"

"Wow, that was so long ago. Bonnie would probably remember it better than I would."

The King will say, "I remember it. You put that money in that box and gave it to me. I've never forgotten it. Look at the first week in March 1994."

"Oh yes, Lord, that's when I was mentioned in *Newsweek* magazine as one of the best religious communicators in the English-speaking world!"

"Well, I don't read those magazines much. They're so inaccurate. No, I was thinking of when you were teaching that day. You were leaving class to go to a meeting, and there was a young woman sitting there. You said, 'How are you doing?' She began to weep. You sat down and she told you that her brother had passed away a couple of days ago and her father a couple of months ago. She found the burden of that grief so heavy that she didn't know if she could bear it. And you didn't know what to say, so you just listened. Remember that?"

"Yeah, I guess I do. I felt so inadequate."

And the King will say, "When you stopped to listen to that woman, you were listening to me, and I have never forgotten it."

> There are going to be a lot of surprises at the judgment. You know all that stuff you put on your résumé? It won't matter much. What will matter will be acts of kindness and compassion.
>
> [a]Haddon W. Robinson, "The Sheep and the Goats" (sermon, Gordon-Conwell Theological Seminary, South Hamilton, MA, March 2011).

Closely related to the technique of dramatization is apostrophe where the speaker addresses an imaginary figure, even an inanimate figure, as when the apostle Paul exclaims, "O death, where is your victory? O death, where is your sting?" This technique also uses the power of indirection. As the listeners overhear the preacher speaking to an "actor" on stage, they listen with shields lowered. After all, the preacher is addressing the "actor," not them. Furthermore, apostrophe shows rather than tells. It depropositionalizes an idea. If you were preaching on materialism, an unadorned statement might sound like this: "Materialism is an idol that tries to supplant God." When clothed in apostrophe, the same idea might sound like this:

> Stand up straight, Mammon, I'm talking to you. Look me in the eye. What makes you think you can tell us what to do? Who put you in charge? You may rule in downtown Singapore, but you do not rule in this church! No one can serve two masters, so we renounce you, Mammon, and we announce our allegiance to the one and only King of kings.

Tapping into imagination, apostrophe is an indirect yet effective way to exhort listeners.

Use testimony. Anna Carter Florence defines testimony as "a narration of events paired with a confession of belief."[24] This includes the story of one's conversion, as in George Whitefield's *Journals*, C. S. Lewis's *Surprised by Joy*, and Augustine's *Confessions*, which he calls his "testimony."[25]

---

[24]Anna Carter Florence, *Preaching As Testimony* (Louisville, KY: Westminster John Knox, 2007), xiii.

[25]George Whitefield, *Journals* (London: Banner of Truth, 1960); C. S. Lewis, *Surprised by Joy: The Shape of My Early Life* (New York: Harcourt, Brace, Jovanovich, 1955); see Amanda Hontz Drury, *Saying is Believing: The Necessity of Testimony in Adolescent Spiritual Development* (Downers Grove, IL: InterVarsity Press, 2015), 149. Drury references Augustine's "Letter to Darius" in *The Confessions*.

It also includes, perhaps primarily includes, narratives of one's daily walk with God. As with other kinds of story, this one employs similar rhetoric: indirection as the speaker talks about his or her headache (not the listeners'), vivid language that uses the "third operation of the mind" to approximate actual experience, emotion coupled with cognition (a dynamic combination), and community building through identification as the listeners realize they are not alone. Furthermore, when delivered well (as discussed in the next chapter), testimony—indeed any story—causes listeners to empathize with the speaker's emotions.

"WHO WILL CONVERT THE WEST?" BY DR. TIMOTHY KELLER

All the rhetorical functions described in this chapter operated in a portion of Timothy Keller's sermon as he spoke about how to be "resilient"—strong and flexible, always springing back to the original shape after being bent or stretched.

Fifteen years ago I did a Bible study with a group of men on the book of Psalms and I came away thinking, "Oh my goodness, I really don't know much about prayer." I had always felt guilty for not praying enough. Then my wife came up with an illustration that went down deep and changed my heart.

She said, "Imagine that the doctors told you that you have a fatal condition and that you're going to die from it. But every night at eleven if you take a pill you'll survive and you'll live for a very long time; but if you ever miss that pill at eleven you'll be dead by morning. Would you ever forget to take the pill? Would you ever say 'Oh, my gosh, I watched that TV show a bit too long, I was playing a video game, now I'm dying.'"

She told me, "We're going to die without prayer; we're not going to make it without prayer. This is the pill." That was the moment I realized, "This is a necessity."[a]

[a]Tim Keller, "Who Will Convert the West?" (sermon, Gordon-Conwell Theological Seminary, South Hamilton, MA, January 27, 2016). See also Timothy Keller, *Prayer: Experiencing Awe and Intimacy with God* (New York: Penguin, 2014), 9-10.

When a remembrancer shares a testimony in a sermon, the story often takes on an analogical quality. That is, the literal events become a metaphor for talking about some aspect of life with God. My story in chapter four of meeting my future mother-in-law for the first time and being "accepted in the beloved" functions that way. Another recounts an experience of spelunking in a cave of western Pennsylvania. The way my friends and I felt our way forward in the black cave became a "confession of belief" about walking with God even in constricting darkness. I'm sure you have your own examples of such stories.

Tony Evans is a master of the analogical testimony. In the same sermon we referenced in the last chapter, he told a story that served as confession of belief.[26] He and his wife were on a cruise to Alaska when a terrible storm broke out. "People were screaming and pianos were rolling!" Tony's wife called the bridge of the ship and relayed an angry message to the captain that he should have avoided this storm, and a few minutes later an assistant sent the captain's reply: "Ma'am, this ship was built with this storm in mind. We knew that there was going to be a day when we would face nature at its most vicious, so way back when we were putting the boat together we contemplated this moment. The storm is bad, but the boat is better." Indeed, the boat is better, and Evans's analogy helped the listeners remember and take heart.

Use stories from history. History—church history in particular—is a vast repository of stories that can rouse memory. Those memories face both inward and outward. That is, a story from church history causes us to look inward by identifying with the main character. We ask ourselves, sometimes without being aware that we are asking, do I have that kind of faith? Stories also help us face outward by reminding us that the faith once delivered is not only personal but also communal. Our fathers and mothers before us placed their faith in Jesus and without them the church might not exist today.

---

[26]Tony Evans, "Building on the Right Foundation," PreachingToday, www.preachingtoday .com/sermons/outlines/2010/july/buildingontherightfoundation.html, accessed April 3, 2017.

THE MARTYRDOM OF POLYCARP

Polycarp was the bishop of Smyrna and his story vivified this truth: "Do not fear what you are about to suffer. . . . Be faithful unto death" (Rev 2:10). I used the story of his martyrdom in a sermon on the church in Smyrna (Rev 2:8-11).

As Polycarp was entering the stadium, the tumult became great. The proconsul sought to persuade him to deny [Christ], saying, "Have respect to thy old age. Swear by Caesar, and I will set thee at liberty. Reproach Christ." Polycarp declared, "Eighty and six years have I served Him, and He never did me any injury: how then can I blaspheme my King and my Savior? Hear me declare with boldness, I am a Christian." The proconsul said, "I have wild beasts at hand; to these will I cast thee." But he answered, "Call them then, for we are not accustomed to repent of what is good in order to adopt what is evil." And again the proconsul said to him, "I will cause thee to be consumed by fire if thou wilt not repent." But Polycarp said, "You threaten me with fire which burns for an hour, but art ignorant of the fire of the coming judgment and of eternal punishment. But why tarriest thou? Bring forth what thou wilt."

While he spoke, he was filled with confidence and joy, and his countenance was full of grace.

The proconsul was astonished, and sent his herald to proclaim in the midst of the stadium three times, "Polycarp has confessed that he is a Christian." And when the funeral pile was ready, Polycarp laid aside his garments. Placing his hands behind him and being bound like a distinguished ram taken out of a great flock for sacrifice, the Bishop looked up to heaven and said, "O Lord God Almighty, the Father of thy beloved and blessed Son Jesus Christ, I give Thee thanks that Thou hast counted me worthy that I should have a part in the number of Thy martyrs, in the cup of thy Christ, unto the resurrection of eternal life. Amen."

When he had pronounced this "amen," those who were appointed for the purpose kindled the fire.[a]

[a]"The Encyclical Epistle of the Church at Smyrna Concerning the Martyrdom of the Holy Polycarp," in John MacArthur Jr., *The MacArthur New Testament Commentary* (Chicago: Moody Press, 1983-2007), electronic version.

Stories from church history can be as ancient as Polycarp or as recent as the history of your own organization. Many pastors find that a yearly vision-casting sermon can draw on the history of the church to remind the congregation of their core values. Stories that capture the essence of the vision inspire like nothing else.

Of course, stories must be delivered well. Verbal content can fall like a wounded duck or rise like a soaring falcon depending on how the nonverbal channel is used. That is our next topic.

6

DELIVERY AS A TOOL FOR STIRRING MEMORY

The brain, without any conscious intent, determines
very early in a sermon whether the mind's lights will come
on or will short out and turn off. The choice of words, the syntax,
the pronunciation, the inflection of the voice and much more will
determine whether the brain decides to tune out or tune in.

RICHARD COX, *REWIRING YOUR PREACHING*

The face is what is most expressive. . . .
It is often equivalent in expressiveness
to what can be said in many words.

QUINTILIAN

Words, words, words! . . .
Is that all you blighters can do?
Don't talk to me of stars shining above;
if you are in love—show me!

ELIZA DOOLITTLE

MR. GRUFFYDD IS THE VILLAGE MINISTER in *How Green Was My Valley* by Richard Llewellyn. The story is set in Wales during Victoria's reign. Mr. Gruffydd's Calvinist chapel is as unadorned as an iceberg but also possesses the angular, clear, and sharp beauty of ice. That is also how he preaches. His words have no frill or padding, yet they possess austere magnificence. His delivery too:

> When Mr. Gruffydd started his sermon, he always put a few sheets of paper on the ledge by the Bible, but never once was he seen to use them. He started to speak as though he were talking to a family, quietly, in a voice not loud, not soft. But presently you would hear a note coming into it, and your hair would go cold at the back. It would drop down and down . . . but then he would throw a rock of sound into the quiet and bring your blood splashing up inside you, and keep it boiling for minutes while the royal thunder of his voice proclaimed the Kingdom of God and the Principality of Christ. . . . That is how we came from Chapel every Sunday re-armed and re-armoured against the world, re-strengthened, and full of fight.[1]

That sounds like the work of a remembrancer. Mr. Gruffydd equipped his congregation through not only what he said but also how he said it—the delivery, the nonverbal component of oral communication. Delivery is what we sound like and look like when we speak. It includes all the elements listeners hear in our voices, such as pronunciation, projection, pitch, rate, and force. It also includes all the elements our audience sees in our deportment: gestures, facial expression, eye contact, and posture. The nonverbal channel holds a primary place, not secondary, in the work of a remembrancer as he or she brings to present consciousness the ancient words of God's book.

DELIVERY: HOW IT WORKS

The nonverbal channel is largely neglected in theorizing about the ministerial arts because to some people it seems unimportant. These

---

[1]Richard Llewellyn, *How Green Was My Valley* (New York: Simon and Schuster, 1939), 165.

people agree that delivery is necessary, but so is a mat to wipe your shoes on. That view of the mat needs to be upgraded because, as oral communication, preaching is incarnational. God has placed his Word in bodies so that we turn ink into blood. The nonverbal channel reinforces, amplifies, clouds, or deconstructs a preacher's words.

Another reason delivery is neglected is that, for some preachers, it smacks of playacting. They fear that a focus on delivery will force them to change their natural ways of speaking. I understand that feeling. Homiletician Ian Pitt-Watson strikes the right note: "Be yourself. We are not professional actors playing the part of a preacher. . . . We have much to learn from the theater, but we are amateurs in this field. Amateur theatricals are embarrassing in the church."[2] We certainly do not want to produce charlatans who take on a stage persona, so this chapter's approach to delivery promotes authenticity, not hucksterism.

Yet another factor that leads to neglect is the difficulty of changing delivery. A riverbed is not easily turned after the years have worn a channel. "What's the use of practicing delivery?" we ask ourselves. "I am who am I, and I speak the way I speak." Once again, I am sympathetic. Patterns are hard to change, but it is worth the effort. Furthermore, as a professor and coach, I have discovered that tangible improvements can be made in as little as one or two practice sessions.

Finally, some roll their eyes at the topic of delivery because they have a skewed opinion of themselves. That is, the sender's perspective does not match the listener's perspective. Then the speaker watches himself or herself on video and gains an audience member's perspective—and pain often follows! We discover that we hunch our shoulders, or speak too quickly, or scowl. The pause that seemed like a Grand Canyon of silence while we were speaking was actually rather short. Of course, sometimes when we watch ourselves we may be pleased by what we see. The nervousness was hardly noticeable, and the moment where our mind went blank did not come across as

---

[2]Ian Pitt-Watson, *A Primer for Preachers* (Grand Rapids: Baker, 1986), 90.

jumbled or protracted. In either case—a view of self that is either too high or too low—some people do not feel the need for training because they are not seated in the pews.

Juxtaposed to these factors that cause homileticians to neglect delivery is the simple fact that people pay attention to the nonverbal channel, consciously or unconsciously, and it influences them. For example, the majority of viewers who watched the famous Kennedy-Nixon debate on television in 1960 rated Kennedy as the winner, but those who listened on radio gave Nixon the nod. On television, Kennedy appeared youthful, confident, and vigorous. He looked straight at the camera, whereas Nixon looked at the questioner. Nixon wore a gray suit that blended into the background, refused to wear makeup, and, most damning of all, occasionally wiped perspiration from his brow when Kennedy pressed him. He appeared shady. But on radio, a medium that privileges ideas more than appearance, he was articulate and convincing.

Humans read nonverbal communication. We are like Clever Hans, the remarkable horse who performed in Germany in the early 1900s. The horse's trainer, Willhelm von Osten, trained Clever Hans to add, subtract, multiply, divide, tell time, keep track of the calendar, differentiate musical tones, and spell. Von Osten might ask the horse, "If the first Tuesday of the month falls on the fifth, what is the date of the following Thursday?" Hans would tap out the number seven with his hoof, and the crowd would gasp. As a result of the firestorm of public interest, the German board of education appointed a commission, known as the "Hans Commission," to investigate von Osten's claims and methods. It concluded that no subterfuge was used in the performances. Then psychologist Oskar Pfungst took over, and he observed that when von Osten knew the answer to the question, Hans got 89 percent of the answers correct, but when von Osten did not know the answer, Hans's score dropped to 6 percent. So Pfungst turned his attention to the trainer and discovered that von Osten gave off extremely subtle, unconscious signals to Hans. As Hans tapped, tension would mount in the trainer and then be released when the horse hit the right number.[3] Von Osten might give a slight smile, change his posture a bit, or exhale in relief.

Horses read nonverbal communication and humans do too. We are hardwired to use and interpret body language. That is the assumption behind the phenomenon of microexpressions. First discovered in 1966, microexpressions are extremely rapid movements of facial muscles arising from underlying emotions. The expressions flash across the face so quickly (lasting only one twenty-fifth of a second), that most dialogue partners do not consciously notice them. However, people with high emotional intelligence, who have intuitive competence in reading people, do pick up on them. Experts at identifying deception are known as "truth wizards."[4] These wizards are rare. In one study of twenty thousand people, only fifty qualified with at least 80 percent accuracy in spotting lies (most people rate around 50 percent). Secret service agents are the most skilled at reading the nuances of the face and body language.

Whereas much nonverbal communication is learned and culture-specific, such as the Filipino "eyebrow flash" (a quick raising of the eyebrows to indicate agreement), Ekman and Friesen spent years reaching the conclusion that six expressions seem to be universal: happiness, sadness, anger, surprise, fear, and disgust. Tribespeople in the mountains of Irian Jaya, businessmen in London, and families in the barrios of Mexico City all look remarkably similar when they express those emotions. Even blind babies make the same faces.[5] Furthermore, some behaviors such as "eye-blocking" are so hardwired that children who are born blind will cover their eyes when they hear

---

[3]The story of Clever Hans can be found in many sources, Oskar Pfungst, *Clever Hans: A Contribution to Experimental Animal and Human Psychology*, trans. C. L. Rahn (New York: Henry Holt, 1907); and David Hothersall, *History of Psychology* (New York: McGraw-Hill, 2004).

[4]For more information about truth wizards, see Pär Granhag and Leid Strömwall, *The Detection of Deception in Forensic Contexts* (Cambridge: University of Cambridge Press, 2004), 269.

[5]Barry Brummett, Linda Putnam, and Richard Crable, *Principles of Human Communication*, 2nd ed. (Dubuque, IA: Kendall Hunt, 1984), 84.

things they don't like.[6] They did not learn this from observation. It is intuitive and natural. If you want to know what the facial expressions look like, look in the mirror as you feel the emotions. Or watch Pixar's 2015 movie *Inside Out*, a film devoted to the themes of memory, emotion, and facial expression. Five animated characters embody five of the six universal emotions.[7]

Similarly, scientists have observed universal gestures and postures related to pride and shame. In studies of judo masters who participated in the 2004 Olympic and Paralympic Games, both sighted and blind athletes from thirty countries used the same body language for pride and shame. For example, arms raised meant victory, and a lowered head and slumped shoulders meant defeat. Researchers concluded that the behaviors came from nature not nurture.[8]

This hardwiring that helps us engage in and interpret nonverbal behaviors may be a survival instinct useful in situations such as the approach of a stranger. We quickly scan the stranger's dress, gait, size, posture, and so forth to determine danger. Or we discern rapidly whether a child sprawled on the ground is in distress or just playing. Determinations like these happen in a flash. As Malcolm Gladwell comments, the process of interpretation is "fast and frugal"; the mind is like "a giant computer that quickly and quietly processes a lot of the data we need in order to keep functioning as human beings."[9] Much of that processing takes place in the limbic system of the brain, the area closely associated with emotion and also with generating and interpreting body language. The fact that people are hardwired for nonverbal communication leads to things we experience daily.

---

[6]Carol Kinsey Goman, *The Silent Language of Leaders: How Body Language Can Help or Hurt How You Lead* (San Francisco: Jossey-Bass, 2011), 88.

[7]*Inside Out*, directed by Pete Docter and Ronnie Del Carmen, (Emeryville, CA: Pixar Animation Studios, 2015). The end credits for *Inside Out* pay tribute to Ekman who served as a consultant.

[8]J. L. Tracy and D. Matsumoto, "The Spontaneous Expression of Pride and Shame: Evidence for Biologically Innate Nonverbal Displays," *Proceedings of the National Academy of Sciences* 105 (2008): 11655-60. In Goman, *Silent Language*, 19-20.

[9]Malcolm Gladwell, *Blink: The Power of Thinking Without Thinking* (New York: Little, Brown and Co., 2005), 11.

When the nonverbal message conflicts with the verbal, listeners trust the nonverbal. Nonverbal communication is difficult to manipulate. It tends to be an accurate reflection of the heart, thus listeners trust it. When the factory of the heart produces verbal communication, a speaker can inspect and alter the words before shipping them out. But when the factory produces nonverbal communication—a posture, facial expression, or excited tone—the speaker places the product in the display window for all to see. If the words say, "Welcome, it's great to see you," but the hands push the congregation away and the brow says, "I wish you weren't here," we believe the latter. If the words say, "I'm fine," but the frowning mouth, flat voice, and averted eyes say otherwise, we doubt the words. In a classic study from the 1960s, Albert Mehrabian studied the phenomenon of mixed messages. He concluded that when speakers conveyed their feelings in an ambiguous way—that is, when their words did not seem to match their delivery—listeners interpreted the speaker's feelings based on facial expression and tone of voice more than words.[10]

Facial Expressions 55%	Voice 38%	Words 7%

Figure 4. Mehrabian's study demonstrates that listeners rely on the face to decipher emotions

Sending mixed messages also confuses listeners. A team of neuroscientists used an electroencephalograph (EEG) to measure the peaks and valleys of brain waves. One valley, dubbed N400, occurs when subjects see gestures that do not tally with the words. This is the same brain wave pattern that occurs when people hear nonsense language.[11] The brain doesn't know what to do with the jumble, so it uses the nonverbal cues as the baseline of interpretation and then tries to

[10] Albert Mehrabian, "Communication Without Words," *Psychology Today* 2 (September 1968), 53.
[11] S. D. Kelly, C. Kravits, and M. Hopking, "Neural Correlates of Bimodal Speech and Gesture Comprehension," *Brain and Language* 89 (2004): 253-60. In Goman, *Silent Language*, 32-33.

harmonize the words with the picture. If the two cannot be harmonized, we distrust the words and the speaker.

When the speaker is a preacher, the ministry of reminding stalls. The words may proclaim a well-known truth such as "We are citizens of heaven," but if the face and tone of voice say, "Who cares?" or "I don't really believe that," memory will not be stirred. The truth will remain buried under the rubble of forgetfulness.

The nonverbal channel is the primary conveyer of relationship and emotion. Communication scholars estimate that 65 percent of social meaning and 93 percent of emotional meaning come through the speakers' appearance, tone of voice, and behavior such as touching (known as *haptics* in communication studies).[12] Through these channels we discern if the relationship is romantic, professional, pastoral, and so forth. Consider the social and emotional meaning embedded in these statements about eye contact:

> Drink to me only with thine eyes, and I will pledge with mine.[13]

> Immediately, while [Peter] was still speaking, the rooster crowed. And the Lord turned and looked at Peter. And Peter remembered the saying of the Lord. . . . And he went out and wept bitterly. (Lk 22:60-62)

The eyes communicate—no doubt about it. With the eyes we pledge, plead, remind, and remonstrate. The eyes also encourage and limit participation, even the "eyes" of a robot. At the 2009 Human-Robot Interaction conference in La Jolla, California, scientists observed how the robot named Robovie used eye contact to guide conversation when two people interacted with it at the same time. The robot played the part of a travel agent, greeting the two guests, introducing itself, and asking about travel plans. When it looked equally at each person, they took turns speaking, but when Robovie made less eye contact with one person, he or she spoke less, and when it completely ignored

---

[12]Randall P. Harrison, "Nonverbal Communication: Exploration into Time, Space, Action, and Object," *Dimensions in Communication*, ed. James H. Campbell and Hal W. Helper (Belmont, CA: Wadsworth, 1965), 161.

[13]Ben Jonson, "Song: To Celia," 1616.

one person, he or she spoke least. Similarly, another team of scientists demonstrated that a robot's "touch," such as patting a shoulder or giving a high-five, encouraged participation.[14]

A fascinating study done at Harvard in the early nineties by Ambady and Rosenthal demonstrates that receivers discern social and emotional meaning through delivery. The sonorous title of their article is "Half a Minute: Predicting Teacher Evaluations from Thin Slices of Nonverbal Behavior and Physical Attractiveness."[15] The researchers showed Harvard undergraduates "thin slices" of video—thirty seconds—of professors lecturing. The sound was turned off or scrambled so that the students observed only body language. Then they were asked to rate the professors on attributes such as "attentive," "dominant," "likeable," "anxious," and "professional." The results were then compared to end-of-the-semester evaluations from another group of students. The second group had spent a semester with the professor in class so they had much more "data" on which to determine their rating. How well did the two sets of evaluations match? "Remarkably well." Ambady and Rosenthal were "amazed and baffled." They then sliced thinner and thinner, getting down to five- and even two-second clips. The results showed only a minor drop in correlation with the end-of-semester evaluations. First impressions about social and emotional meaning materialize in a flash in the limbic system.

Ambady and colleagues performed a similar experiment with surgeons talking to their patients, this time using only audio.[16] They set out to see if they could predict which surgeons were likely to be sued for malpractice based simply on the surgeons' tone of voice as they interacted with patients. Taped conversations were filtered so that the words

[14]Kristina Grifantini, "Making Robots Give the Right Glances," *MIT Technology Review,* March 11, 2009, www.technologyreview.com/s/412490/making-robots-give-the-right-glances.

[15]Nalini Ambady and Robert Rosenthal, "Half a Minute: Predicting Teacher Evaluations from Thin Slices of Nonverbal Behavior and Physical Attractiveness," *Journal of Personality and Social Psychology* 64, no. 3 (1993): 431-41.

[16]Nalini Ambady, et al., "Surgeons' Tone of Voice: A Clue to Malpractice History," *Surgery* 132, no. 1 (2002): 5-9; in Gladwell, *Blink,* 42-43.

were unintelligible but vocal qualities such as pitch, intonation, and rhythm were discernable. The researchers asked an independent group of listeners to rate the surgeons on qualities similar to the ones used with the professors: "hostility," "warmth," "dominance," and "anxiousness." Using only those ratings, the researchers were able to accurately predict which surgeons were later sued for malpractice. It turns out that patients rarely sue surgeons they like, even if the surgeon has made a mistake, and "liking" is greatly influenced by tone of voice. It would be interesting to see these studies replicated with preachers. How do preachers use tone of voice and body language to convey social and emotional meaning?

Nonverbal behavior generates emotion in the sender. One of the most surprising findings in studies of nonverbal communication is that delivery not only reflects the speaker's emotion, it also generates it. Delivery is both chicken and egg, perhaps because God has made the body and heart as a holistic unit.

Paul Ekman, the scientist who identified the universal facial expressions, spent years mapping the face, and he stumbled across the truth that emotions follow the body.[17] When he and his colleagues practiced activating their own facial muscles to produce various expressions of sadness, they were "stunned" to discover that "expression alone is sufficient to create marked changes in the autonomic nervous system." These expressions generated actual sadness, anguish, and anger with heart rate rising and hands becoming hot along with other physiological changes. Ekman, Friesen, and Levenson (with follow-up experiments by a German team) painstakingly documented this effect with control groups. Participants were instructed to make various faces, and then the team measured physiological changes associated with stress.[18] Their conclusions were consistent—the face not only manifests emotion like steam escaping the lid of a boiling pot, it also heats the pot. Furthermore, most germane to the topic of this book, delivery heats not only the speaker's pot but also the listeners.' What temperature does your delivery create in those who listen to you?

---

[17]The story and quotation are in Gladwell, *Blink*, 207.
[18]Gladwell, *Blink*, 206-8.

The speaker's delivery prompts a reciprocal response in the listener. Rhetorician and preacher Hugh Blair put it this way: "There is an obvious contagion among the passions."[19] There is nothing new in that insight, all effective preachers, public speakers, and performers experience it, yet few have been able to explain why it happens. Around 380 BC Plato tried to do so in one of his dialogues. In this dialogue Socrates converses with Ion, a rhapsode (singer/reciter), who relates the thrill of reciting Homer before an audience: "At the tale of pity, my eyes are filled with tears, and when I speak of horrors, my hair stands on end and my heart throbs." Ion then describes how his emotion spreads to the audience: "I look down upon them from the stage, and behold the various emotions of pity, wonder, sternness stamped upon their countenances."[20] Ion is exhilarated when this occurs but clueless about why it happens, so Socrates explains that the muse inspired Homer, then Homer inspired the rhapsode, then the rhapsode inspired the audience. The muse is like a magnet that transmits its power through a succession of iron rings to the spectators.

Modern psychology uses the term "empathy" to explain, as Plato might say, this "magnetism." When a sender experiences fear, joy, or another emotion, he or she exhibits those feelings through delivery. Receivers then perceive the feelings, and the perception triggers the same emotion in them.

Neuroscience goes a step further to explain the phenomenon of "mirror neurons," specialized nerve cells in the brain that fire when we see someone perform an action. These cells help people mirror or mimic the actions of the sender, as when a mother smiles at her baby and the baby smiles back. Mirror neurons aid learning, and they also aid empathy. They fire when a receiver perceives emotion in the sender and cause a reciprocal response. For that reason the neurons are of special interest in the study of autism, a disorder that hinders the

---

[19]Hugh Blair, *Lectures on Rhetoric and Belles Lettres*, quoted in Lester Thonssen and A. Craig Baird, *Speech Criticism: The Development of Standards for Rhetorical Appraisal* (New York: Ronald, 1948), 364.

[20]Plato, *Ion*, trans. Benjamin Jowett, classics.mit.edu/Plato/ion.html.

ability to mimic and empathize. For our purposes, mirror neurons are the physiological basis of the contagion. Reviewing scientific research on mirror neurons and emotion, neurologist Richard Restak concludes, "Emotions are infectious. . . . You can catch the mood of other people just by sitting in the same room with them."[21]

Restak could have been describing the *claques* of European theaters and opera houses in the seventeenth through early twentieth centuries. A claque was an organized group of claqueurs—people hired by the manager to laugh, weep, request encores, or otherwise give the audience a shot of adrenaline so they would respond. Today's claques can be heard on sitcoms with their recorded laugh tracks. These communication venues—theater and sitcoms—know the power of the contagion, even if they use it only for vain or pecuniary motives.

In contrast, ministers are interested in mirror neurons because they seek to stir latent memories through the "law of instinctive sympathy," the preacher's "right arm in the work of persuasion."[22] As we have seen, activating memory involves cognition, but just as importantly it also involves emotion. The most influential sender of non-verbal messages, the person who is most contagious, is the pastor. Emotion flows downhill.

Picture an occasion when the memory function of preaching takes center stage, such as Christmas, Easter, or even a run-of-the-mill Sunday when the text "merely" repeats a well-known truth. With Mr. Gruffydd, ministers want to "re-arm, re-armour, and re-strengthen" the congregation against the world with the foundational truths of the faith: God sent Jesus in the fullness of time; God raised Jesus who now sits at his Father's right hand; the church is a family; out of the heart flow the issues of life; heaven is the Christian's hope. Truths like these could garner a shrug and a yawn, yet they are crucial in forming a Christian mind so we want to deliver them well. We do not want our

---

[21]Richard Restak, *The Naked Brain: How the Emerging Neurosociety is Changing How We Live, Work, and Love* (New York: Three Rivers, 2006), 103.

[22]Robert L. Dabney, *Sacred Rhetoric or a Course of Lectures on Preaching*, February 1870, www.onthewing.org/user/Dabney%20-%20Sacred%20Rhetoric.pdf.

sermons to be, as Ralph Waldo Emerson described his own lectures, "fine things, pretty things, wise things, but no arrows, no axes, no nectar, no growling, no transpiercing, no loving, no enchantment."[23]

DELIVERY: HOW TO WORK IT

Speech teachers find it difficult to coach nonverbal communication through the medium of print because delivery is something seen and heard. When described in writing delivery is mummified, but the exercises that follow give you the opportunity to practice aloud. Even with live coaching, the subtle components of nonverbal communication, such as voice inflection and facial expression, are difficult to coach. This is because a direct channel runs between the heart, voice, and face. A teacher can suggest and demonstrate techniques, but for those techniques to match the emotional state of the student, the student must actually feel the emotion. That is difficult to coach!

Take smiling as an example: while it is possible to manipulate a lips-only smile with the zygomatic major (the muscles around the lips), it is nearly impossible to manufacture a smile of true enjoyment. That kind of smile subtly contracts the muscles around the eyes (the orbicularis oculi) and raises the cheeks to produce crow's-feet at the edge of the eyes. That facial landmark even has a name—Duchenne's marker—named after the nineteenth-century French neurologist Duchenne de Boulogne, who wrote about the two kinds of smiles: "The first obeys the will, but the second is only put in play by the sweet emotions of the soul."[24] Out of the heart proceed words, and I believe that the same truth applies to body language—out of the heart the body responds.

The Frenchman's statement points to an all-important principle of delivery—to stir others, you must first be stirred.[25] You can go no

---

[23]In David L. Larsen, *Anatomy of Preaching: Identifying the Issues in Preaching Today* (Grand Rapids: Kregel, 1989), 71.

[24]In Patrick O'Neill, "Understanding the Science of the Smile," *The Oregonian* (Jan. 14, 2001): L14.

[25]For a thorough discussion of delivery, including a video demonstration of nonverbal skills, see Jeffrey D. Arthurs, *Devote Yourself to the Public Reading of Scripture: The Transforming Power of the Well-Spoken Word* (Grand Rapids: Kregel, 2012).

further in the art of delivery if this principle is missing, and in many ways if it is present, you need go no further.

Start with yourself. The first person to wade into the waters of memory should be the preacher, and then he or she beckons the covenant community from the depths. To remind the church that they have been born again into living hope (1 Pet 1:3), immerse yourself in that hope. To remind the church that they should not worry about life—what we eat, or drink, or wear—remind yourself how God cares for the birds of the air and that you are more valuable than they (Mt 6:25-27). Before preaching on the three hallelujahs of Revelation 19, shout, "Hallelujah!" at least three times! A reservoir can dispense only what it contains.

The necessity of starting with ourselves places a rigorous demand on the spiritual life of the minister, and no shortcut will serve. Only by Bible study, prayer, and meditation can our own hearts be magnetized to the lodestone, which is God himself. Augustine, a professional rhetorician who defended the use of rhetoric for Christian proclamation, kept first things first: the preacher "should be in no doubt that any ability he has . . . derives more from his devotion to prayer than his dedication to oratory; . . . he must become a man of prayer before becoming a man of words."[26]

Ministers need to keep themselves "in the love of God" (Jude 21). That verse does not mean God's love has sprung a leak and we must stay at the pumps to keep it afloat. Rather, it implies that *we* have sprung a leak. The context shows what Jude had in mind: "Building yourselves up in your most holy faith and praying in the Holy Spirit, keep yourselves in the love of God, waiting for the mercy of our Lord Jesus Christ that leads to eternal life" (Jude 20-21). Prayer is one of the means by which we build ourselves up and persevere in the faith, thus keeping ourselves in the love of God. Another way to conceive of the command to "keep yourself" is "remember him." That is what Paul commanded Timothy: "Remember Jesus Christ, risen from the dead, the offspring of David, as preached in my gospel" (2 Tim 2:8). And still another way

---

[26] Augustine, *On Christian Teaching,* 4.14.

is implied in the phrase "strengthen yourself in the Lord." David did that after he returned with his men from a raid and discovered that the Amalekites had burned his village and taken captive all the women and children. The men wept until they had strength to weep no more, and then they turned on David and threatened to stone him! Then comes this: "But David strengthened himself in the LORD his God" (1 Sam 30:6). Perhaps he composed a psalm or sang to the Lord. Certainly he prayed, reminding himself of the promises and character of his God.

On February 21, 1836, Robert Murray McCheyne, the great nineteenth-century pastor from Scotland, recorded this in his diary:

> Preached twice in Larbert, on the righteousness of God, Rom. i. 16. In the morning was more engaged in preparing the head than the heart. This has frequently been my error, and I have always felt the evil of it, especially in prayer. Reform it, then, O Lord.

On March 5 he wrote:

> Preached in Larbert with very much comfort, owing chiefly to my remedying the error of 21st Feb. Therefore the heart and the mouth were full. "Enlarge my heart, and I shall run," said David. "Enlarge my heart and I shall preach."[27]

McCheyne gives us a vivid example of how we can be strengthened in the Lord.

It will take a lifetime to learn these disciplines—it is certainly taking me a lifetime!—but stay at it. The result will be what Spurgeon called *earnestness*—an exposition of the Word marked by the conviction that comes from proven experience and sincere belief.[28] When the minister displays genuine earnestness, the congregation follows. The believers who gather for worship often arrive with personal burdens, minds wandering and hearts drifting. Preaching as reminding gathers those hearts around the hearth of our own earnestness.

---

[27]In Andrew Bonar, *The Life and Remains, Letters, Lectures, and Poems of the Rev. Robert Murray McCheyne* (New York: Robert Carter, 1847), 39.

[28]C. H. Spurgeon, *Lectures to My Students* (Grand Rapids: Baker, 1977), 2:145-62.

So start with yourself. Pray and meditate deep into the Word. No technique can replace that. Without it, no technique will avail. Teaching someone to display the marks of earnestness without the heart of earnestness is like painting a furnace red to make it appear hot, or like the Wizard of Oz spinning dials and cranking levers to discharge flames to distract attention from the man behind the curtain.

To add yet another metaphor, one from the world of dog sledding, the speed of the leader is the speed of the team. Because of the law of sympathy, empathy, contagion, magnetism—call it what you will—the congregation keeps pace with the preacher. Social science verifies that truth, but theology lies under it. God has placed in the heart of the sheep a desire to be shepherded. To be sure, some sheep bite and some go astray, but in every believer is the life of Christ, a life that is humble and submissive, tuned to hear the shepherd's voice and eager to walk in his ways. Believers want to follow a friend, mentor, leader—a pastor—who practices what he or she preaches. We gravitate to leaders who lead.

STRENGTHEN YOURSELF IN THE LORD

How can we strengthen ourselves in the Lord? Here are some suggestions.

- Have regular devotions unrelated to sermon preparation and ministerial duties. Try praying the Scriptures back to God, starting with the Bible's own "prayer book": Psalms.
- Develop a spiritual friendship with someone who will feed your soul rather than drain it.
- Ask God for a mentor, someone who will speak the truth in love.
- Sing. By expressing truth with affect and art, music penetrates the heart.
- Take Sabbath. Rest, worship, play, recharge.

Once the foundation of a vibrant devotional life is in place, we can build with techniques to construct solid delivery.

Observe, but don't mimic, preachers you admire. If you listen to one preacher you admire, you will become a poor imitation, but if you listen to multiple preachers, you can take elements from each and weave them into the fabric of your own style. My own practice is to listen to seven to ten sermons by a well-known preacher and then move on to another set of sermons by another preacher. I download the sermons to my portable device and listen while I drive or exercise. My most recent preachers were Fred Craddock and Martyn Lloyd-Jones. From Craddock I was reminded of the power of story, humor, and induction. His sermons were delightful. From Lloyd-Jones I gained inspiration and skill in the use of language—what precision and directness! I also upgraded my ability to think and preach theologically. Lloyd-Jones was an expositor, but he also brought a theological-thematic mindset to each text. And in terms of delivery, he embodied his own definition of preaching: "Logic on fire! Eloquent reason!"[29] In addition to listening to preachers, you may like to listen to Scripture readers, paying attention to how they use their voices to convey the emotions percolating in each text.[30]

Watch yourself on video. Video is the great schoolmaster. Painful though it can be, video shows us what the congregation sees and hears. As stated earlier, we often have a skewed perception of ourselves. When asked if they considered their preaching "energetic," 43 percent of pastors responded "yes," but only 29 percent of congregations said "yes." When asked if they felt their preaching was "conversational," the numbers were similar: 46 percent of pastors agreed versus 22 percent of congregants.[31]

Try recording yourself on video as you preach or read aloud. Then give yourself a candid critique on projection, gestures, eye contact, posture, facial expressions, vocal variety, and earnestness. When you see a weak point, contemplate what needs to change.

---

[29]D. Martyn Lloyd-Jones, *Preaching and Preachers* (Grand Rapids: Zondervan, 1971), 97.
[30]My favorite Scripture reader is Hunter Barnes, pastor and professional actor. See www.daily radiobible.com. See also www.dailyaudiobible.com, www.bhpublishinggroup.com, and professional actor David Suchet on www.biblegateway.com.
[31]Eric Reed, "The Preaching Report Card," *Leadership Journal*, Summer 1999, www.ctlibrary .com/le/1999/summer/9l3082.html.

RECORD YOURSELF AS YOU READ

Read aloud the following passage, a portion of a sermon by Dr. Patricia Batten, and record yourself on video. Then use the checklist below to evaluate your delivery. These paragraphs call for pauses, changes of rate, and direct and compassionate eye contact. They likely call for few gestures because the mood is subdued, but make those gestures count.

Maybe you've had your own Psalm 73 moments when you've doubted God's goodness.

Look at how the wicked prosper. Look at some of the people who don't acknowledge God. For many of them, life is a breeze. . . . No worries of money or health. They live by the motto "Me first you last." They get things done by way of force and oppression, and God does nothing. . . . But for so many who follow God, the wind never seems to be at their backs. Their worries are too many and their paychecks too small. They don't sail in carefree winds. . . . They just hope they make it back to shore. . . .

Lately, as Asaph headed to work, cymbals in hand, he didn't feel like making music. Because as he headed down the dusty roads of Jerusalem, all he could see was grief. His path clouded by dust and his minded dusted with doubt, Asaph wondered, "Where is God?" And maybe you've wondered that same question, "Where is God?"[a]

Checklist

☐ I project my voice. Although this passage conveys sadness and worry, I can still be heard and understood easily.

☐ I use my hands and body to gesture appropriately. This passage calls for few gestures, so when I use one, I make it count.

☐ My face matches the verbal content, creating empathy in the listener.

☐ I use vocal variety (volume, rate, and pause). In this exercise, pause helps convey mood—I am not afraid of silence.

☐ I am earnest. I have used my imagination to empathize with Asaph so that my own empathy will magnetize the listeners to Psalm 73.

[a]Patricia Batten, "The Story of a Worship Leader Who Lost His Song," in *Models for Biblical Preaching: Expository Sermons from the Old Testament*, eds. Haddon W. Robinson and Patricia Patten (Grand Rapids: Baker, 2014), 61-70.

Speak extemporaneously. The term *extemporaneous* means that the sermon is well prepared, usually delivered from skeletal notes, but is not read word for word from extensive notes.[32] I recommend extemporaneous delivery because "paper is a very poor conductor of electricity."[33] The paper isolates you from your listeners and prevents the contagion from spreading; the paper weakens the flow of magnetic force.

Reading a sermon from sheets of paper greatly hinders nearly every aspect of nonverbal communication covered in this chapter, particularly eye contact, gestures, and variety of rate. When most people read aloud, their voices flatten and fall into a cadence dictated by the eyes scanning the page, rather than lively thoughts arising from the heart. A metronome belongs in the piano studio, not the pulpit.

If you find yourself overly dependent on notes, some simple techniques can help you wean yourself from paper. Many preachers find it helpful to write out a manuscript but not preach from it. Some of the wording of the manuscript will seep into the oral sermon, thus gaining the benefits of precision and creativity without incurring the liabilities of stilted, formal, and abstract language common to writing. If you do not carry a manuscript to the pulpit, what should you carry? Try skeletal notes. This can be as small as a Post-It note or as large as one letter-size sheet of paper, but no more than this. Develop your own system of marks, colors, and symbols to make the notes easy to use in oral delivery.

Another aid to memory is making your main points logically simple with a flow such as problem-solution-result, cause-effect, contrast (not this, but this), or chronology (past-present-future). These natural modes of thought work well as the skeleton of a sermon because when points flow in an organic, simple order, the preacher remembers them easily and the listeners comprehend them effortlessly.

[32]For a thorough discussion of the strengths and weaknesses of various modes of delivery, see Jeffrey Arthurs, "No Notes, Lots of Notes, Brief Notes," in *The Art and Craft of Biblical Preaching: A Comprehensive Resource for Today's Communicators*, eds. Haddon Robinson and Craig Brian Larson (Grand Rapids: Zondervan, 2005): 600-606.
[33]Wayne McDill, *The Moment of Truth* (Nashville: B & H, 1999), 145.

Finally, don't forget to practice. For your practice sessions, first read your manuscript aloud, then set it aside and preach from the single page of notes. Afterward, take stock of places you forgot or jumbled. Ask yourself if the flow of thought needs to be simplified. Is the mental path clear and well marked so that the bloodhound does not leave the trail to chase a rabbit?

Get your body and voice involved. Walk to the pulpit with purpose. Remember that the communication of earnestness starts before you begin to speak. Smile (if appropriate), establish eye contact, and then begin. Remember that the voice follows the body, so fire up your body and let your voice express your natural emotional state.

ENGAGING BODY AND VOICE FOR EFFECTIVE COMMUNICATION

The following exercises are intended to help you engage some of the strategies discussed in this chapter.

Using Gestures

As Hamlet advised the troupe of actors, "Suit the action to the word," or as Spurgeon said, "Let the gesture tally with the words, and be a sort of running commentary and practical exegesis upon what you are saying."[a] Use gestures as you say these lines aloud:

- When God calls us, he empowers us, and he sends us.

- No! It won't work. The children of Israel already tried it.

- There are two factors to consider: first, your faith, and second, your influence.

- It was about this long and this high.

- Will you respond? Will you say yes? Behold, he stands at the door knocking. Will you open?

- Psalm 73 is a poem about doubt, confusion, and pain, but it is also a poem of faith. It's the story of a fellow named Asaph, and it's also our story.

Engage Your Voice

Recognizing the power of voice to awaken empathy, project authority, and convey sincerity, consider how one interjection—"Oh!"—can convey thought and mood. Say that word aloud to convey the meanings in the parentheses. Remember to activate your face and hands because the voice follows the body.

- Pity. (You have just learned that your friend did not get the new job.)

- Shock. (How could the interviewers be so blind as to choose the other candidate?)

- Anger. (They didn't hire you because you are over fifty? That's against the law!)

- Understanding. (Their decision actually has nothing to do with age; it is because you are overqualified.)

- Delight. (Wait! They changed their mind. You've been hired!)

- Wariness. (Your friend asks for a loan until he receives his first paycheck.)

Convey Various Meanings by Emphasizing Different Words

Use your voice—pitch, force, and pause—to convey the various meanings found in parentheses. Although the wording of the sentence is identical in all eight reiterations, the meaning should change each time.[b]

- *I* never said she stole my purse. (Maybe someone else said it.)

- I *never* said she stole my purse. (I didn't say it before and I'm not saying it now.)

- I never *said* she stole my purse. (Maybe I implied it.)

- I never said *she* stole my purse. (It was someone else altogether.)

- I never said she *stole* my purse. (Now that I think of it she might have just borrowed it.)

- I never said she stole *my* purse. (But she did steal someone else's.)

- I never said she stole my *purse*. (It was my wallet I was complaining about.)

Putting It All Together

Use your voice, gestures, eye contact, and facial expression to convey the indicated meaning and mood:

- Contentment: "The Lord is my shepherd, I shall not want."

- Doxology: "The heavens declare the glory of God, and the sky above proclaims his handiwork."

- Pleading: "Let me not be put to shame, for I take refuge in you."

- Confidence: "The Lord is my light and my salvation; whom shall I fear?"

- Anger: "Contend, O Lord, with those who contend with me; fight against those who fight against me!"

- Scoffing: "Transgression speaks to the wicked deep in his heart; there is no fear of God before his eyes."

- Assurance: "Fret not yourself because of evildoers; be not envious of wrongdoers. For they will soon fade like the grass and wither like the green herb."

- Steadfastness: "I said, 'I will guard my ways, that I might not sin with my tongue.'"

- Delight: "Clap your hands, all peoples! Shout to God with loud songs of joy!"

[a]Spurgeon, *Lectures to My Students*, vol. 2, 115.
[b]Adapted from Jana M. Childers, *Performing the Word: Preaching as Theater* (Nashville: Abingdon, 1998), 85. Also used in Arthurs, *Devote Yourself*, 101-2.

7

CEREMONY AND SYMBOL
AS TOOLS FOR
STIRRING MEMORY

In every generation a person is
duty-bound to regard himself
as if he personally has gone forth from Egypt.

MO'ED PESAHIM 10:5E

●

REMEMBER JIMMIE, Dr. Sacks's patient who had Korsakov's syndrome?[1] Jimmie had no short-term memory and was caught in a time warp, believing in 1975 that he was still a sailor in World War II. He spent his days wandering the halls of Dr. Sacks's clinic, adrift, but then the doctor happened to observe Jimmie in chapel receiving Holy Communion. His face, eyes, and body showed unmistakable signs of attention, steadiness of comprehension, and alignment of mental and emotional energies. Sacks describes the scene:

> Fully, intensely, quietly, in the quietude of absolute concentration and
> attention, he entered and partook of the Holy Communion. He was
> wholly held. . . . There was no Korsakov's then, nor did it seem possible
> or imaginable that there should be; for he was no longer at the mercy

---

[1]Oliver Sacks, *The Man Who Mistook His Wife for a Hat and Other Clinical Tales* (New York: Harper and Row, 1987), 23-42. I have paraphrased and quoted from those pages.

of a faulty and fallible mechanism—that of meaningless sequences and memory traces—but was absorbed in an act, an act of his whole being, which carried feeling and meaning in an organic continuity and unity.[2]

This is the power of ceremony and symbol—Holy Communion, in particular—for the ministry of reminding: reconnecting feeling and meaning to the core tenets of our faith. Jimmie epitomizes all of us spiritually. Prone to wander, likely to forget our identity and the covenant to which we are called, we need something tangible to pull us back. So we eat and drink "in remembrance." The minister's primary means of reminding the faithful is preaching, using the rhetorical arts of style, story, and delivery, but we also use ceremony and symbol—liturgical arts—to keep the truth warm in heart and mind.

CEREMONY AND SYMBOL: HOW THEY WORK

In ancient Israel, continuity with the past was nurtured by a vast network of ceremony and symbol. The sacrifices of animals and grain, the abstention of leaven from bread, the landscape dotted with altars and stones of remembrance, the rhythm of the day, week, and year, broken regularly with prayers and ceremonies—all these drummed a ceaseless cadence that exhorted the covenant people to remember and not forget.

Just as modern societies erect monuments and shrines to help citizens remember their history and values, so did ancient Israel. As a covenant community, their markers concerned the great acts of God as well as their own vows to obey their Sovereign. Joshua is a case study in the building of those markers. Piles of stone commemorated events such as crossing the Jordan River dry-footed (Josh 4:1-24), Achan's apostasy and the trouble it brought on Israel (Josh 7:25-26), and victory over the king of Ai (Josh 8:29; see also Josh 8:30-35; 22:10-34; 24:26-28). In all of these, the overt or subtle purpose was to remind the nation of God's gracious covenant and their obligations to obey the covenant stipulations.

---

[2]Ibid., 36.

As we saw in chapter four, sensory experience is the most powerful operation of the mind for riveting attention and compelling belief. Memory of sensory experience is next in efficacy, and imagination of sensory experience, often prompted by discourse, is third. Ceremony and symbol use the top operation—actual sensory experience—to reinforce what is already known and believed. Leaders, ministers, and educators have long known that effective communication requires as much sensory input as possible.

The senses have been thought of as gates into the brain, and modern neuroscience is confirming that. The use of multiple senses not only increases attention, comprehension, and retention when learning something for the first time, it does the same when actualizing something for the second, third, or eighth time. For example, the sense of smell has direct neural connections to the limbic system of the brain, the center of emotion and memory. Odors spark feelings and associations, and when an odor such as incense symbolizes something sacred it serves as a "neuropsychological bridge" that spans time, relationships, and circumstances in ways words cannot.[3]

Sacred spaces. These have the power to re-narrate defining moments and connect people to the ideas, values, and emotions associated with those moments and the spaces where they occurred. Psalm 137 demonstrates this, or rather demonstrates what happens when one is displaced from a sacred space—the holy city of Jerusalem. Writing in exile in Babylon, the poet weeps when he remembers Zion and feels unable to "sing the LORD's song in a foreign land" (Ps 137:4). This was more than homesickness. It arose from a psychological and spiritual dynamic at play with physical space.

Sacred time. The liturgical year was used as a reminder of salvation history, not simply as the marking of the calendar. Whether it was the weekly keeping of Sabbath to remember God as creator (Ex 20:8-11) or the yearly festivals of Passover, Booths, and Firstfruits to remember God as deliverer and sustainer (Ex 23:14-17), or the Day of

---

[3]Richard H. Cox, *Rewiring Your Preaching: How the Brain Processes Sermons* (Downers Grove, IL: InterVarsity Press, 2012), 139.

Atonement wherein the people remembered their sins and afflicted themselves (Lev 16:1-34; 23:26-32; Num 29:7-11), sacred time added its voice to the chorus of Israelite worship with each commemoration helping the worshiper to remember God and all his benefits. The liturgical year also served as a tool to transmit the essentials of the covenant to succeeding generations, passing the faith from parents to children: "When your children say to you, 'What do you mean by this service [Passover]?' you shall say, 'It is the sacrifice of the LORD's Passover, for he passed over the houses of the people of Israel in Egypt'" (Ex 12:26-27). The liturgical year is a means of proclaiming that God has been our help in ages past and is also our hope for years to come.

Rituals. Sensory, physical acts of worship carry immense power to ignite individual and communal memory. Incense burned, oil anointed, hands laid, knees bent, rams' horns sounded, bitter herbs tasted, firstborn redeemed, processions fluttering, and the smoke of offerings ascending are sacred performances that enact theology, bringing close what is distant. The simple ritual of holding out one's hands to receive the bread of communion can actualize the belief that we come to God as supplicants, beggars all. Nothing in our hands we bring, simply to thy cross we cling.

Other symbols. Things like the tablets of the law placed beside the throne of the king (Deut 17:14-20) served as visual reminders of the covenant and its stipulations. Doorframes and gates bore the words of God so that memory was stirred at each coming and going (Deut 6:9). Clothing and accoutrements, from tassels (Num 15:37-41) to phylacteries (Deut 11:18), reminded people of their identity. Even topography, the way the mountains surrounded Jerusalem, reminded the psalmist of God's watch care (Ps 125:2).

In an unexpected twist on the need to remember, which we normally associate with fallible humans who stray, the "stones of remembrance" set on the shoulders of the high priest as well as his breastplate bearing the names of the tribes of Israel reminded *God* of his covenant people

(Ex 28:12, 29).[4] The priests embodied intercession, bringing the nation before God, calling him to remember his people. Isaiah 62:6-7 is similar: the "watchmen" were to "put the LORD in remembrance . . . and give him no rest until he establishes Jerusalem and makes it a praise in the earth." Similarly, in 1 Chronicles 16:4 David appointed Levites to "invoke, to thank, and to praise the LORD." The word for "invoke" is from *zakar*. They were to "bring to mind"—to God's mind!—his promises.

Public reading of Scripture. This also keeps the covenant fresh. Many readings were performed in conjunction with Passover and the Festival of Booths. At other times ministers conducted special seasons of reading when renewal was needed, as when Joshua prepared the people to enter the Promised Land (Josh 8:30-35) or when Josiah rediscovered the Law and called all the people "both small and great" to hear the priests read "all the words of the Book of the Covenant" (2 Kings 23:2). The early church continued the pattern of regular reading as Paul commanded Timothy to devote himself to the public reading (1 Tim 4:13). In the mid-second century the pattern continued, as evidenced by Justin Martyr's comment that in their services folk gathered to hear the Scriptures read "as long as time permits."[5] In the ancient world public reading was crucial because of illiteracy and the scarcity of texts, but the need is just as great today. Even though most believers in the West can read any of the multiple copies of the Bible they own, only a minority do so regularly.

Music. The singing of psalms, hymns, and spiritual songs is another engine to power memory (Col 3:16). Deuteronomy 31:19-22 is interesting in this regard. As Moses approached death, the Lord

---

[4]The "memorial portions" of offerings also had this function—reminding God of his covenant. See Lev 2:2; 5:12; 6:15; 24:7; Num 5:26. Of special interest is Acts 10:4 where the prayers and alms of Cornelius, the God-fearing Gentile, "ascended as a memorial before God," perhaps reminding God of his promise to bring Gentiles into the covenant.

[5]Justin Martyr, *1 Apology* 67, in Timothy J. Ralston, "Scripture Reading in Worship: An Indispensable Symbol of Covenant Renewal," in *Authentic Worship: Hearing Scripture's Voice, Applying Its Truths*, Herbert W. Bateman IV, ed. (Grand Rapids: Kregel, 2012), 208. By the end of the fourth century the dominant liturgical pattern included three readings, and some lectionaries in Mesopotamia had four or six lessons. To see the pattern continued in the Reformation and early American Puritanism, see Jeffrey D. Arthurs, *Devote Yourself to the Public Reading: The Transforming Power of the Well-Spoken Word* (Grand Rapids: Kregel, 2012), 26-27.

gave him a song to remind the nation by summarizing the history of the covenant and warning of severe curses for forgetting that covenant. The Lord says to Moses, "This song shall confront them as a witness (for it will live unforgotten in the mouths of their off-spring)." Words that are sung lodge in memory better than words that are simply spoken.

Awareness of that commonsense phenomenon may have prompted Martin Luther to compose "German psalms" for the untaught and illiterate people in his charge. His goal was that the Word of God might be "kept alive among them by singing."[6] Similarly, John Calvin translated into metrical French all 150 psalms, the Ten Command-ments, and the Song of Simeon. He did this to make the texts stick in the hearts of his people.[7] Likewise John Wesley collected, translated, and published hymns to serve as a "body of experimental and prac-tical divinity" for the newborn movement called Methodism, and his brother Charles helped the Methodists learn doctrine by writing more than six thousand hymns.[8] I've turned my own hand to hymn writing, taking as a theme 2 Timothy 2:8. You can find that hymn, "We Remember Jesus Christ," in the appendix of this book.

Besides being easy to memorize, words that are sung add an emotive element to statements of doctrine. The Bible's prayer book, the book of Psalms, is also its hymnbook. Although he was not writing about psalms or hymns, Plato's words ring true: "Rhythm and harmony find their way into the inward places of the soul, on which they mightily fasten, imparting grace."[9] Music opens the heart like nothing else.

Writing his own psalm, Habakkuk recounted history—God's mighty hand in the exodus—and then applied the truth of the Al-mighty's omnipotence and faithfulness to his own crisis as the Chal-deans bore down on little Israel:

---

[6]Quoted in Marianne H. Micks, *The Future Present: The Phenomenon of Christian Worship* (New York: Seabury, 1970), 63.

[7]James K. A. Smith, *Imagining the Kingdom: How Worship Works* (Grand Rapids: Baker, 2013), 175.

[8]Bernard L. Manning, *The Hymns of Wesley and Watts* (Eugene, OR: Wipf and Stock, 1942), 12.

[9]Plato, *The Republic*, 3, theoryofmusic.wordpress.com/2008/04/music-in-platos-republic.

Though the fig tree should not blossom,
    nor fruit be on the vines,
the produce of the olive fail
    and the fields yield no food . . .
yet I will rejoice in the LORD;
    I will take joy in the God of my salvation. (Hab 3:17-18)

To stabilize his emotions in the present and chart a course for the future, Habakkuk wrote of the Lord's past faithfulness.

Singing corporately creates a synergistic experience that unites and sustains participants such as those who took part in the Civil Rights Movement. Protestors sang, chanted, and marched their way to equality.[10] Similarly, one of my friends attended the Promise Keepers' Stand in the Gap event at the National Mall in Washington, DC, in 1997. He described the overwhelming inspiration of hearing seven hundred thousand men singing "O for a thousand tongues to sing my great Redeemer's praise." The synergistic function of singing also operated with my wife and her six siblings, a much smaller group, as they sang hymns at the deathbed of their beloved mother, Ruth Hansen. It was a quintessential instance of the use of music to remind each other of the promises of God, his lovingkindness that never fades, and the solidarity of family. Strength for today and bright hope for tomorrow.

Before moving to a discussion of methodology, it might be helpful to address a question: Isn't the biblical emphasis on ceremony and symbol isolated to the Old Testament? To what extent should the church build its theology and practice of worship on Israelite customs? Behind these questions is an awareness that the church is not Israel and that Christ has instituted a new covenant. I acknowledge the differences between the old and new covenants. God has revealed himself more fully in Christ in the new covenant, and our great high priest has fulfilled the law. Sacrifices are no longer required because Jesus has made the ultimate offering—himself—"once for all" (Heb 10:1-14).

---

[10]See R. B. Van Naaren et al., "Mimicry and Prosocial Behavior," *Psychological Science* 15, no. 1 (2009): 71-74; and Charles J. Stewart, Craig Allen Smith, and Robert E. Denton Jr., *Persuasion in Social Movements*, 2nd ed. (Prospect Heights, IL: Waveland, 1989), 213-32.

God's presence on earth has shifted from the Temple to individual believers (1 Cor 6:19) and the corporate church (Eph 2:21-22). The law, including its ceremonial prescriptions such as washings, sacrifices, and festivals, was a shadow (Heb 8:5), but now the substance has come. The church still makes offerings, but now these are the fruit of lips that acknowledge his name, doing good, and sharing, "for such sacrifices are pleasing to God" (Heb 13:15-16).

Having acknowledged that the new is not the old, we also recognize the continuity between covenants. Nothing has changed in the nature of God and basic principles of how to approach him in worship. Worship was and is a whole-person response to God's revelation. Gratitude, praise, awe, fear, obedience, confession, and celebration are timeless modes of worship even though most Old Testament forms are no longer prescribed. Memory plays a crucial role in whole-person response, and ceremony and symbol aid memory.

The New Testament contains remarkably little information about the forms of corporate worship. This silence can be interpreted as an abandoning of form, with cultural or personal styles ruling the day, or the silence may indicate that widespread practices made a discussion of worship unnecessary.[11] We have hints in Acts and the Epistles that the second scenario is more likely.[12] Acts 13:2 is one of those hints: the church at Antioch was praying, "worshiping" the Lord. The word is *leitourgeo*, from which we get the English word *liturgy*. A literal rendition might be "they were doing the liturgy," likely using the form of a synagogue service—prayers, reading of Scripture, teaching, and hymns—with the addition of a new element, the Lord's Supper. Even the new element had roots in an old element—the Passover.

[11]Timothy J. Ralston, "'Remember' and Worship: The Mandate and the Means," *Reformation and Revival* 9, no. 3 (Summer 2000): 77-89.

[12]See Ronald P. Byars, *What Language Shall I Borrow? The Bible and Christian Worship* (Grand Rapids: Eerdmans, 2008), 49; Marianne H. Micks, *The Future Present: The Phenomenon of Christian Worship* (New York: Seabury, 1970), 6-9; and Charles P. Price, "Remembering and Forgetting in the Old Testament and Its Bearing on the Early Christian Eucharist" (ThD diss., Union Theological Seminary, 1962), 320-39.

The template of a New Testament service probably consisted of four parts: gathering, the Word, the Eucharist, and sending. That pattern is millennia old.[13] Assuming that we want to follow the four parts today, plenty of room exists for contextualization. From the exuberance and spontaneity of a Pentecostal meeting in Puerto Rico to the reverent hush of a liturgical Good Friday service in Cambridge, England, to the African churches dancing their offerings down the aisle, we have a wide latitude of freedom.[14] Interspersed into the four parts are three "elements," as Ralph Martin identifies them, that flesh out the template: a "charismatic element" of enthusiastic praise and prayer under the guidance of the Spirit, a "didactic element" of teaching, and a "eucharistic element" of prayer, hymns, and the Lord's Table.[15]

The most explicit New Testament instruction on ceremony is found in the four passages on the Lord's Supper (Mt 26:26-29; Mk 14:22-25; Lk 22:14-20; and 1 Cor 11:23-26). All four carry forward the Old Testament's preponderant emphasis on memory in worship. In the pre-Nicene church (prior to AD 325) the Eucharist was thought of as the "Christian Passover."[16] After an exhaustive historical and theological study, Charles P. Price states, "The Eucharist is a memorial of the Christ-event in the same sense that the Passover meal is a memorial of the deliverance from Egypt. There is no need to look outside the institutions of old Israel for the roots of new Israel."[17] Those roots budded and flowered and Holy Communion became the ceremony of remembrance par excellence. Although both ceremonies use bread, blood, and table fellowship to commemorate redemption, in Christ we have a more

---

[13]Bryan Chapell provides a helpful chart that lays out, side by side, the liturgies of Rome (pre-1570), Luther (ca. 1526), Calvin (ca. 1542), Westminster (ca. 1645), and a modern approach offered by liturgist Robert G. Rayburn (ca. 1980) in *Christ-Centered Worship: Letting the Gospel Shape Our Practice* (Grand Rapids: Baker, 2009), 23-24.

[14]I believe that even ministers who follow the "regulative principle" of Reformed worship, which states that God "may not be worshiped according to the imaginations and devices of men . . . or in any other way not prescribed in the Holy Scriptures" ("Westminster Confession of Faith," 21.1), will be able to use the following suggestions.

[15]Ralph P. Martin, *Worship in the Early Church* (Grand Rapids: Eerdmans, 1975), 132-33. The book of Acts and the Epistles seem consistent with this set of components. See Acts 2:42, 46; 1 Cor 11:17-21; 14:26-31; Col 3:16.

[16]Sykes, "The Eucharist as 'Anamnesis,'" 118.

[17]Price, "Remembering and Forgetting in the Old Testament," 313.

precious lamb, a greater rescue from a greater threat, and an exodus that will carry us not only out of Egypt but into eternal life. The ceremony deserves a central place in corporate worship because we have received it directly from the mouth of our Lord, and it will not cease in this age.[18]

CEREMONY AND SYMBOL: HOW TO WORK THEM

To effectively stir memory with ceremony and symbol, ministers need to fire up the "doxological imagination" of the congregation. That is John Davis's term for worship as "a holistic and embodied human activity" that utilizes cognition, imagination, emotion, will, and body to help worshipers recognize that God is really among them (1 Cor 14:25).[19] Davis's approach to "real presence" is harmonious with the biblical theology of memory presented in this book. Memory conflates the past, present, and future into what Davis calls "kingdom time" so that worshipers truly (but not physically) stand at the Red Sea to witness the hand of God, run with Peter and John to see the tomb empty, and stand on the mountain with the disciples to see the Lord ascend. The spell of modernism, with its dogged insistence that physical and empirical reality is the only reality, must be broken.

Davis argues that the Protestant zeal to guard against the excesses of sacramentalism has resulted in a theology of real absence. We talk about God, but our roots in frontier revivalism, with its emphasis on human experience and decision, places the worship leader and preacher, the architects of experience, in the spotlight. Remembrancers are aware of that tendency and strive to open the eyes of the congregation so that in worship they experience the real (though unseen) presence of the triune God. As Hebrews states, in worship we "come to Mount Zion and to the city of the living God,

---

[18]The ceremony certainly had a central place in the early church. Clement, Igantius, the *Didache*, and Justin Martyr indicate that Holy Communion was served consistently in public worship. Ralston states that for fifteen hundred years "there is no record of Sunday gathering of Christians that did not include the celebration of the Lord's Table." Ralston, "'Remember' and Worship," 82.

[19]John Jefferson Davis, *Worship and the Reality of God: An Evangelical Theology of Real Presence* (Downers Grove, IL: InterVarsity Press, 2010), 78, 86-97.

the heavenly Jerusalem, and to innumerable angels in festal gathering, and to the assembly of the firstborn who are enrolled in heaven, and to God, the judge of all" (Heb 12:22-23).[20] These spiritual realities are not currently experienced with the senses, but they are, nevertheless, realities.

If you belong to the low church tradition, your challenge is to transcend a conversational, even chatty, approach to worship to jolt folks with the reminder that God is present, and if you belong to the high church, your challenge is to use prescribed and sometimes dusty forms to do the same.

DO YOUR RITUALS HAVE MEANING?

This checklist might help you evaluate your church's rituals:[a]

☐ Can we articulate a biblically informed rationale for our intentional rituals?

☐ How do our rituals connect us, meaningfully, to the one apostolic church of the past and present?

☐ How do our rituals reinforce or undermine the vision and values of the congregation?

☐ Are our rituals, in the eyes of most congregants, filled with meaning? Do the worshipers know what the rituals represent?

☐ Are the rituals accessible to children, youth, and others who might need special help in understanding them?

☐ Do the rituals engage the heart?

☐ Which rituals need refreshing? How might you accomplish this?

☐ Should any rituals be abandoned or altered?

[a]Gary A. Parrett and S. Steve Kang, *Teaching the Faith, Forming the Faithful: A Biblical Vision for Education in the Church* (Downers Grove, IL: InterVarsity Press, 2009), 329.

---

[20]Other Scriptures also indicate real (but not physical) presence when the church gathers: 1 Cor 5:4; 14:23-25; Mt 18:20; 28:20.

Join proclamation with visualization. This is a regular pattern in Scripture. After the debacle and subsequent victory at Ai, Joshua built an altar to commemorate the events, but lest the people forget that defeat or victory result from forgetting or remembering the covenant, he wrote on the altar a copy of the law of Moses, and afterward he read all the words of the Law: "There was not a word of all that Moses commanded that Joshua did not read before all the assembly" (Josh 8:30-35). Another instance of joining proclamation with ceremony is our Lord's institution of the new covenant. He did so with symbolic gestures—taking, blessing, breaking, and distributing bread—and he explained those gestures with words. Likewise, when God delivered the Jews through Mordecai and Esther, they established a new holiday (a "holy-day") called Purim. The meaning of Purim was "recorded in writing" and the "Jews firmly obligated themselves and their offspring . . . that without fail they would keep these two days according to what was written" (Esther 9:26-32). Future generations did not have to decipher the meaning of Purim because the ceremonies came with their own theological commentary. Nonverbal symbolism augmented by verbal explanation garners fruit from both kinds of communication—emotion-inducing, holistic, experiential participation, along with the conceptual precision and clarity of written and spoken words.[21]

Most ministers join proclamation and visualization when performing the two primary rites of the Christian church—the Lord's Supper and baptism. The same practice can also occur with other elements of a service such as taking the offering. We should not assume that the act of giving automatically registers in hearts as an act of worship. When taking the offering, try using words like these:

> Every man shall give as he is able, according to the blessing of the LORD your God that he has given you. (Deut 16:17)

---

[21]Recall the incident of the bronze serpent (Num 21; 2 Kings 18) discussed in chapter two. The symbol void of explanation became empty, formal religion at best, idolatry at worst.

Do not neglect to do good and to share what you have, for such sacrifices are pleasing to God. (Heb 13:16)

Honor the LORD with your wealth
   and with the firstfruits of all your produce. (Prov 3:9)

Those words can be expanded, as needed, to teach, cast vision, and inspire.

Devote yourself to the public reading. That was Paul's command to Timothy and by extension to ministers today. The word "devote" means to "hold the mind toward," "concentrate on," or "apply oneself to." Timothy was to "practice" public reading of Scripture, "immerse" himself in it, and "persist" in it (1 Tim 4:13-16). Unfortunately, some churches with a high view of the inspiration and authority of Scripture do not obey the command. In fact, I have wondered if there is an inverse relationship—the higher the view of Scripture, the lower the practice of reading it aloud. High orthodoxy, low orthopraxy.

Public reading is indispensable in the work of reconnecting the faithful to their faith. That has been true since the beginning, that is, since the Word was first inscripturated. The generation of Jews that came out of Egypt experienced the mighty hand of God that gave birth to Israel as a nation, but their children did not see those events (Deut 11); therefore, God spoke to future generations through periodic readings of the covenant (Deut 17:18-20; 27:3-8; 31:9-13). Stirred by public reading, memory maintained the continuity of Israel, blessing and warning those who heard. Early in church history, the importance of reading the Word led to a cluster of ceremonies such as carrying the Bible in procession, chanting it, reading from a special location, and having people stand when listening. Could practices like these be contextualized in your church?

Most importantly, for public reading to stir memory, it must be read well, but once again, our orthopraxy often fails. Who has not heard the Scriptures read in a way that conveys insecurity, boredom, or glibness? That was the case in Mark Twain's day too: "The average clergyman could not fire into his congregation with a shotgun and hit a worse reader than himself. . . . I am not meaning to be flippant and irreverent, I am only meaning to be truthful. The average clergyman, in all countries and of all denominations, is a very bad reader."[22] So practice your reading. Model the skills discussed in the previous chapter and also train others.[23]

One way to devote ourselves to the public reading is by weaving Scripture into other portions of the service such as the offering, as we discussed above. Another place could be the opening of the service when the leader greets the people and calls them to worship. Scripture is a perfect tool for reminding the faith family of the character and promises of God, pointing the arrows of their expectation toward the theme for the day.[24] Compare the opening sentences in Table 1.

Table 1. Opening sentences of a worship service

Uhm, Okay . . . how's everyone doing? Pretty good? Good. We're gonna worship, so maybe you could stand?	I greet you in the name of the Lord. Let us come before him with thanksgiving and extol him with music. (Ps 95:2)
Good morning. I said *gooood morning!* Welcome to _____ church. Wow! I can feel the energy in this room. Wow! Here we go!	Good morning. Welcome to _____ church. We've gathered to praise the Lord, learn about him, and, as Scripture says, to encourage one another and build each other up. (1 Thess 5:11)
We're going to start now, so could everybody please take their seats? There's plenty of room up front.	As we begin, remember the promise of God: The Lord is near to all who call on him, to all who call on him in truth. Seek the Lord while he may be found; call upon him while he is near. (Ps 145:18 and Is 55:6)
You know, life can be pretty tough. Know what I mean? So, that's why we have come this morning. Because, you know, life is hard. So, be encouraged. Let's sing.	Our help is in the name of the Lord, who made heaven and earth. (Ps 124:8)

Source: Inspired by the British satirical website Ship of Fools (shipoffools.com), which regularly sends an "intrepid mystery worshiper" to various churches to report on the proceedings. Summarized in Debra Rienstra and Ron Rienstra, *Worship Words: Discipling Language for Faithful Ministry* (Grand Rapids: Baker Academic, 2009), 48.

---

[22]Mark Twain, *A Tramp Abroad*, vol. 2 (Hartford: American, 1880), 92 in Robert G. Jacks, *Getting the Word Across: Speech Communication for Pastors and Lay Leaders* (Grand Rapids: Eerdmans, 1995), 11.

[23]See my book *Devote Yourself to the Public Reading of Scripture* where you can find many suggestions on how to leverage this important tool of reminding.

[24]Two excellent resources for weaving Scripture into every element of the service are *The Worship Sourcebook*, eds. Emily R. Brink and John D. Witvliet (Grand Rapids: Baker, 2004); and Chapell, *Christ-Centered Worship*.

What ministry of reminding takes place in the first column? Life is hard and the front seats are empty. Conversely, the second column has the potential to minister to people who arrive distracted and discouraged, perhaps the majority of people who attend our services, so leverage the first words they hear to stir memory and ignite faith. Do the same with the final words too—the benediction or closing (see table 2).

Table 2. Final words of a worship service

Thanks for coming, everyone. Hope you have a great day. See you next week.	The Lord bless you and keep you; the Lord make his face to shine upon you and be gracious to you; the Lord lift up his countenance upon you and give you peace. (Num 6:24-26)
Dear Lord, thanks for being with us, and please help us remember the meeting that takes place right after this service downstairs in the fellowship hall. Amen.	Please stand for charge: Whatever you do, whether in word or deed, do it all in the name of the Lord Jesus, giving thanks to God the Father through him. (Col 3:17)
Dear Lord, we pray that you'll help us remember the sermon today, the main point Jack made, that we should, like, take hope in you and not let anything get us down. Amen.	May God, who has been our help in ages past, And who is our hope for years to come, Be your guard while troubles last, And lead you to his eternal throne (from Isaac Watt's hymn, based on Psalm 90).
Go eat yogurt! Note: I did *not* make this up. A neophyte worship leader with a vivacious personality but no training, came to the end of the service and realized he needed to dismiss the people. Not wanting to sound like an elementary school teacher ("You are dismissed") he blurted out . . .	May the God of peace be with you all. Amen. (Rom 15:33)

Another way to devote ourselves to public reading is with confessional statements such as the Apostles' Creed or Nicene Creed. These are theological distillations of much Scripture. Their primary memory function is ideational, but when led with verve they also spark emotion. When I was pastoring in the low-church tradition—very low—I introduced the Apostles' Creed to my congregation. I updated some of the language to make it accessible, and we began with a ten-minute teaching on the creed. The people loved it! Similarly, as dean of the chapel at a multidenominational seminary, I created a creedal affirmation for our whole community:

We believe in God the Father:
> Creator, Sustainer, Lawgiver, Redeemer, and Judge. He is over all,
> and through all, and in all.

We believe in Jesus Christ, his only begotten Son:
> he is the resurrection and the life. Whoever believes in him has
> eternal life.

We believe in the Holy Spirit:
> sent from the Father, he baptizes, fills, seals, guides, and graces the
> Church.

Father, Son, and Spirit:
> from everlasting to everlasting, Amen.

The seminary community was used to the recitation of such creeds, and they also responded positively.

Uphold the Lord's Supper. This is the supreme ceremony of remembrance for children of the new covenant. Although theological positions abound—their name is legion—the positions share some common ground:

- *As memorial* ("do this in remembrance of me"). Remembrancers help people be re-membered to the death of the Lord Jesus.

- *As Eucharist* ("thanksgiving"). This was the term used in the early church; remembrancers can help people give thanks.

- *As eschatological banquet* ("I will not eat it until it is fulfilled in the kingdom of God," Luke 22:16, 18). Remembrancers remind the people that he will return and the kingdom that is not yet shall be.[25]

- *As proclamation* ("you proclaim the Lord's death until he comes," 1 Cor 11:26). Remembrancers help people realize that the eucharistic ceremony is nonverbal communication, a tangible parable.

- *As koinōnia* ("fellowship/participation," 1 Cor 10:16-17). Remembrancers help unify the people.

---

[25]Miroslav Volf states, "Memory of God's promise . . . does not describe what *was* or what *is*; it states what the one who is making the promise *will bring about.*" *The End of Remembering: Remembering Rightly in a Violent World* (Grand Rapids: Eerdmans, 2006), 102.

CELEBRATING THE LORD'S SUPPER

Here are some specific suggestions for celebrating the Lord's Supper. If particular convictions or church cultures do not permit all of the suggestions, perhaps they can spark your creativity to find your own way to help folks remember the broken body and spilled blood of our Lord.

Memorial

- Preach on the atonement and follow with the Lord's Supper.

- Read the Gospel texts, 1 Corinthians 11, Isaiah 53, or other texts about the sacrifice of our Lord. Find a way to make the familiar words and ideas "present." For example, try a group reading, simply provide the words for folks to read silently, or accompany the reading with music or artwork.

- Include a creedal affirmation.

Eucharist

- Use a group Scripture reading of thanks to God. Perhaps make it responsive or antiphonal.

- Ask for testimonies of thanks.

- Sing psalms, hymns, and spiritual songs of thanks. Perhaps sing as people are receiving the bread and wine.

- Lift hands or kneel as postures of thanks. The heart follows the body.

Koinōnia

- Serve one another.

- Join communion with a foot washing ceremony.

- As people come forward to receive the bread and wine, address them by name: "Janie, Christ died for you. Chinsoo, Jesus poured out his blood for you."

- Take an offering for someone in the church who is down and out.

- Give an opportunity to confess sins and make peace with each other.

- Eat a meal together and include the Lord's Supper as part of the gathering.

- Read Scripture on the church's unity such as Ephesians 4:1-6.

Eschatological Banquet

- Include the ancient and biblical word "Maranatha!" Come, Lord Jesus!
- Preach on heaven. This is a major biblical theme and motivation for perseverance and holy living, but notably lacking in the pulpit.
- Read Scripture related to hope, the Lord's return, or the coming kingdom.
- Eat a meal together—a feast—as a foretaste and tangible reminder of the things yet to come.

Proclamation

- Preach about the death or return of Jesus. Proclaim!
- Read Scripture about the same.
- Sing about the same.
- Lead the people to do their own proclamation with a responsive reading, creedal affirmation, or other form of hearty heralding.

Inevitably, the topic of the Lord's Supper raises the question of frequency. Scripture simply says, "As often as you eat this bread and drink the cup" (1 Cor 11:26). My own preference is weekly because of the practice implied in Scripture (1 Cor 11:17-20), the habit of the ancient church,[26] and an appreciation for the power of the ceremony to stir memory. But we have no right to measure orthodoxy or piety by frequency.

Uphold baptism. This is the second rite of the church universally practiced through the ages, and like the Lord's Supper, it too has an abundance of theological interpretations. Most of the suggestions above such as employing Scripture readings and songs are appropriate for most theological positions and cultural preferences on baptism. The important thing is to give the people being baptized (or their sponsors) the opportunity to affirm their faith. Thus they serve as their own remembrancers by recounting the mercies of the Lord and his

---

[26]For example the *Didache*, a manual for the organization and conduct of the church written around the end of the first century, states, "Every Lord's day, gather yourselves together, and break bread, and give thanksgiving." 14.1.

life-changing power. This can be done by having the person being baptized share his or her testimony or by leading that person in a short litany of affirmation. Perhaps include the ancient words, "Do you renounce Satan? And all his works? And all his promises?" The witnesses of the baptism will recall their own conversions and the goodness of the Lord in instituting a new covenant. Another aspect of baptism to be rehearsed is its function as initiation into the church. Accompanying baptism with ceremonies that emphasize welcome are appropriate, such as eating together, greeting the baptized in a "receiving line" as at a wedding, affirming the church covenant, and praying for one another.

Remember that in public prayer you are a remembrancer. When a pastor leads in prayer, he or she embodies the theology, values, and ethos of the church. The pastor also actualizes memory. We can draw worshipers from the undertow of the world to breathe again life-giving truths about God even as we address God in prayer. Perhaps this is why many of the prayers in the Bible speak at length *about* God while making supplication *to* God. For instance, in David's prayer to dedicate the building materials for the temple (1 Chron 29:10-19), I estimate that 50 percent of the prayer rehearses who God is: "blessed," "the God of Israel our father, forever and ever," "all things come from you," the one who "tests the heart and has pleasure in uprightness," and so forth. The prayer also states who we are in relation to God: strangers and sojourners, "our days on earth are like a shadow," and so on. Remembrancers take every opportunity, including public prayer, to remind the body of who God is and who they are.

COLLECTS FROM THE BOOK OF COMMON PRAYER

The Book of Common Prayer follows the biblical pattern—first speaking *about* God, then making requests *to* God. Take two examples of collects. The first is a supplication for a person in affliction and the second a thanksgiving for rain. I have italicized the words that recall the attributes and purposes of God. In the first prayer this is more than a third of the words, and in the second more than half.

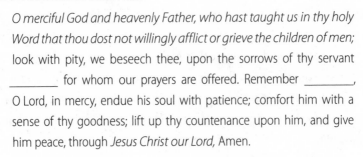

> *O merciful God and heavenly Father, who hast taught us in thy holy*
> *Word that thou dost not willingly afflict or grieve the children of men;*
> look with pity, we beseech thee, upon the sorrows of thy servant
> _____ for whom our prayers are offered. Remember _____,
> O Lord, in mercy, endue his soul with patience; comfort him with a
> sense of thy goodness; lift up thy countenance upon him, and give
> him peace, through *Jesus Christ our Lord,* Amen.

> *O God, our heavenly Father, by whose gracious providence the*
> *former and the latter rain descend upon the earth, that it may bring*
> *forth fruit for the use of man;* we give thee humble thanks that it has
> pleased thee to send us rain to our great comfort, and to the glory of
> thy holy Name; through *Jesus Christ our Lord,* Amen.

To serve as a remembrancer when praying, try addressing God with
a divine name or description congruent with the content of the prayer.
Thus: "Mighty God, we need your power to overcome . . . ." "God who
knows and who provides, our brothers and sisters in Cambodia are in
crisis. . . ."[27] Similarly, the minister could use a comparison: "God,
you have told us that you are like a shepherd who searches for the lost
sheep, so we intercede for our sister. . . . " Our public prayers name
God, and the best names are the ones he has revealed in his Word. The
book of Psalms provides a wealth of examples for us:

- A shield about me (Ps 3:3)
- My King and my God (Ps 5:2)
- Righteous God (Ps 7:9)
- LORD, the Most High (Ps 7:17)
- Rock, fortress, shield, stronghold (Ps 18:2)
- Helper (Ps 54:4)

---

[27]See Debra Rienstra and Ron Rienstra, *Worship Words: Discipling Language for Faithful Ministry* (Grand Rapids: Baker Academic, 2009), 156, for a thorough list of names of God used in the Bible.

- Lord God of hosts (Ps 59:5)
- God of our salvation (Ps 65:5)
- Hope (Ps 71:5)
- Holy One of Israel (Ps 71:22)
- God of vengeance (Ps 94:1)
- Judge of the earth (Ps 94:2)
- King (Ps 99:4)
- God of heaven (Ps 136:26)

The book of Psalms encourages us by example to expand our theological vocabulary when addressing the divine one.

Another tool for public prayer is the "collect form"—you, who, do, to.[28] First, address God with a Scriptural name (you), then acknowledge what that title implies regarding the prayer being made (who), then make an appeal (do), then articulate the result expected in faith (to).

Perhaps the best prayers echo the words of Scripture.[29] By paraphrasing God's Word, the minister disciples the congregation in how to pray and reminds them of what they have heard before. Similarly, the words of a hymn can be the basis for meaningful public prayer, as recommended above: "O God, you have been our help in ages past. . . . "

My final suggestion for public prayer is to engage the worshipers. This could be as simple as prompting them to say "amen" at the end or at various points in the prayer. That was the practice of Israel and the early church. The Coptic Church has the tradition of shouting after the prayer of consecration, "We believe and testify and give praise."

Ceremony and symbol stand at the intersection of emotion, volition, and imagination. Remembrancers throughout history have known this and have used liturgy to stir memory for the glory of God and the good of the people.

---

[28]Ibid., 159.

[29]A helpful resource designed for private devotions can also be used for public prayers. See Kenneth Boa, *Handbook to Prayer: Praying Scripture Back to God* (Atlanta: Trinity House, 1993).

CONCLUSION

•

ST. MUNGO FOUNDED THE CITY OF GLASGOW, Scotland, in the late sixth century. A line from one of his sermons became the unofficial motto of the city and was inscribed on the bell of the historic Tron Church in 1631: "Let Glasgow flourish by the preaching of thy Word and the praise of thy people." In 1866 a shortened secular version became the official motto and today adorns the city's coat of arms: "Let Glasgow Flourish." Visit Scotland's largest metropolis and you will see that motto on buildings, lampposts, clock towers, gates, even rubbish bins. The modern motto expresses a wish that is positive and hopeful yet a bit vacuous. The older motto grounds the hope of flourishing in the means of flourishing—robust preaching and worship.

My wish is that your ministry would indeed flourish—surge, expand, and grow like a tree planted by streams of water—and that this would occur through the power of God's transforming Word, ministered by a faithful remembrancer.

Now, unto him who remembers his covenant and his people,
Who sees our going out and our coming in,
Who hears the prayers of those who cry, "Remember me!"
Who collects our tears in his bottle and writes our trials in his book,
Unto this One—Father, Son, and Spirit—
who inscribes our names on his hands:
May he bring all that he has commanded
and promised to your remembrance,
As you bring those things to the remembrance of your people.
You are the Lord's remembrancer.
Amen.

APPENDIX

We Remember Jesus Christ

19 Dmin7   F/G   Amin   C/E To Coda F   F/G

Cra - dled in   a   stall   Cra - dled in a -
Son   be-came   a - ccursed.   The Son   be-came   a -
Spi - rit   I   will send.   My Spi - rit   I   will
wipe all tears and sighs.   He'll

22 1.-2. C   F/C   3. C   C C/E F

stall.   send.   He has come. He has
ccursed.   cresc. _ _ _ _ _ _ _

27 C/E   Dmin   F   G   C/E   F

died.   He was raised a-gain   to life.   Now He reigns en-throned a -

31 E7   E7/G♯   Amin   B♭2   F/G4   F/A G/B
                                                   2   2 D.C. al Coda

bove on hea - ven's   throne,   soon to re - turn.

Dmin7   F/G   Amin C/E   Dmin7   F/G   C

wipe al tears and sighs.   He'll wi-pe all tears and sighs.

5   F/C   G/C   F/C   C
                 rall.

© 2016 Jeffrey Arthurs & Jonathan Ottaway ALL RIGHTS RESERVED

BIBLIOGRAPHY

Aamodt, Sandra, and Sam Wang. *Welcome to Your Brain: Why You Lose your Car Keys but Never Forget How to Drive and Other Puzzles of Everyday Life.* New York: Bloomsbury, 2008.

Adams, Jay E. *Sense Appeal in the Sermons of Charles Haddon Spurgeon.* Vol. 1 of *Studies in Preaching.* Nutley, NJ: Presbyterian and Reformed, 1976.

Ambady, Nalini, and Robert Rosenthal. "Half a Minute: Predicting Teacher Evaluations from Thin Slices of Nonverbal Behavior and Physical Attractiveness." *Journal of Personality and Social Psychology* 64, no. 3 (1993): 431-441.

Ambady, Nalini, et al., "Surgeons' Tone of Voice: A Clue to Malpractice History." *Surgery* 132, no. 1 (2002): 5-9.

Andrewes, Lancelot. *Lancelot Andrewes and His Private Devotions.* Translated by Alexander Whyte. Grand Rapids: Baker, 1981.

Aristotle, *The Rhetoric and Poetics of Aristotle.* Translated by W. Rhys Roberts. New York: Modern Library, 1954.

Arthurs, Jeffrey D. *Devote Yourself to the Public Reading of Scripture: The Transforming Power of the Well-Spoken Word.* Grand Rapids: Kregel, 2012.

———. "No Notes, Lots of Notes, Brief Notes," in *The Art and Craft of Biblical Preaching: A Comprehensive Resource for Today's Communicators.* Edited by Haddon Robinson and Craig Brian Larson. Grand Rapids: Zondervan, 2005.

———. *Preaching With Variety: How to Re-create the Dynamics of Biblical Genres.* Grand Rapids: Kregel, 2007.

Arthurs, Jeffrey D., and Andrew Gurevich. "Theological and Rhetorical Perspectives on Self-Disclosure in Preaching." *Bibliotheca Sacra* 157 (April–June 2000): 215-26.

Augustine. *Confessions.* Translated and edited by Albert C. Outler. faculty. georgetown.edu/jod/augustine/conf.pdf.

———. *On Christian Teaching.* Translated and edited by R. P. H. Green. Oxford: Oxford University Press, 1997.

Bacon, Francis. *Selected Writings of Francis Bacon.* Edited by Hugh C. Dick (New York: Modern Library, 1955).

Baddeley, Alan. *Your Memory: A User's Guide.* New York: Macmillan, 2004.

Bartlett, F. C. *Remembering: A Study in Experimental and Social Psychology.* Cambridge: Cambridge University Press, 1932.

Batten, Patricia. *Models for Biblical Preaching: Expository Sermons from the Old Testament.* Edited by Haddon W. Robinson and Patricia Patten. Grand Rapids: Baker Academic, 2014.

Blair, Edward P. "An Appeal to Remembrance: The Memory Motif in Deuteronomy." *Interpretation* 15 (1961): 41-47.

Bonar, Andrew. *The Life and Remains, Letters, Lectures, and Poems of the Rev. Robert Murray McCheyne.* New York: Robert Carter, 1847.

Brueggemann, Walter. *Hopeful Imagination: Prophetic Voices in Exile.* Philadelphia: Fortress, 1986.

Brummett, Barry, Linda Putnam, and Richard Crable. *Principles of Human Communication.* 2nd ed. Dubuque, IA: Kendall Hunt, 1984.

Burke, Kenneth. *Counter-Statement.* Berkeley: University of California Press, 1968.

———. *Language as Symbolic Action: Essays on Life, Literature, and Method.* Berkeley: University of California Press, 1966.

———. *A Rhetoric of Motives.* Berkeley: University of California Press, 1969.

Byars, Ronald P. *What Language Shall I Borrow? The Bible and Christian Worship.* Grand Rapids: Eerdmans, 2008.

Calvin, John. *Institutes of the Christian Religion.* Edited by John T. McNeill. Translated by F. L. Battles. Louisville, KY: Westminster John Knox, 1960.

Campbell, George. *Philosophy of Rhetoric.* Edited by Lloyd Bitzer. Carbondale: Southern Illinois University Press, 1988.

Carr, Nicholas G. *The Shallows: What the Internet Is Doing to Our Brains.* New York: W. W. Norton, 2010.

Chapell, Bryan. *Christ-Centered Worship: Letting the Gospel Shape Our Practice*. Grand Rapids: Baker Academic, 2009.

———. *Using Illustrations to Preach with Power*. Rev. ed. Wheaton, IL: Crossway, 2005.

Childers, Jana M. *Performing the Word: Preaching as Theater*. Nashville: Abingdon, 1998.

Childs, Brevard S. *Memory and Tradition in Israel*. Studies in Biblical Theology 37. Naperville, IL: Allenson, 1962.

Cicero. *On the Orator*. Translated by H. Rackam. Edited by Jeffrey Henderson. Cambridge, MA: Harvard University Press, 1942.

Cosand, J. Robert. "The Theology of Remembrance in the Cultus of Israel." PhD diss., Trinity Evangelical Divinity School, 1995.

Cox, Richard H. *Rewiring Your Preaching: How the Brain Processes Sermons*. Downers Grove, IL: InterVarsity Press, 2012.

Craddock, Fred B. *Overhearing the Gospel*, rev. and exp. ed. St. Louis: Chalice, 2002.

Crites, Stephen. "The Narrative Quality of Experience." *Journal of the American Academy of Religion* 39, no. 3 (1971): 291-311.

Dabney, Robert L. *Sacred Rhetoric or a Course of Lectures on Preaching*. 1870. www.onthewing.org/user/Dabney%20-%20Sacred%20Rhetoric.pdf.

Dante. *The Divine Comedy*. Translated by Louis Biancolli. New York: Washington Square, 1968.

Darwin, Charles. *Life and Letters of Charles Darwin*. New York: D. Appleton and Co., 1911.

Davis, Ellen F. *Imagination Shaped: Old Testament Preaching in the Anglican Tradition*. Valley Forge, PA: Trinity, 1995.

Davis, John Jefferson. *Worship and the Reality of God: An Evangelical Theology of Real Presence*. Downers Grove, IL: InterVarsity Press, 2010.

Dickinson, Emily. *The Complete Poems of Emily Dickinson*. Edited by Thomas H. Johnson. Boston: Little, Brown and Co., 1960.

Drury, Amanda Hontz. *Saying is Believing: The Necessity of Testimony in Adolescent Spiritual Development*. Downers Grove, IL: InterVarsity Press, 2015.

Edwards, Jonathan. *Treatise Concerning the Religious Affections*. Vol. 2 of *The Works of Jonathan Edwards*. New Haven, CT: Yale University Press, 1959.

Eliot, T. S. "Burnt Norton." *Four Quarters*. www.coldbacon.com/poems/fq.html.

Galli, Mark, and Craig Brian Larson. *Preaching That Connects: Using Journalistic Techniques to Add Impact.* Grand Rapids: Zondervan, 1994.

Gladwell, Malcolm. *The Power of Thinking Without Thinking.* New York: Little, Brown, 2005.

Goman, Carol Kinsey. *The Silent Language of Leaders: How Body Language Can Help or Hurt How You Lead.* San Francisco: Jossey-Bass, 2011.

Gordon, T. David. *Why Johnny Can't Preach: The Media Have Shaped the Messengers.* Phillipsburg, NJ: P&R, 2009.

Grifantini, Kristina. "Making Robots Give the Right Glances." *MIT Technology Review* (March 11, 2009), www.technologyreview.com/s/412490/making-robots-give-the-right-glances.

Guinness, Os. *Fool's Talk: Recovering the Art of Christian Persuasion.* Downers Grove, IL: InterVarsity Press, 2015.

Harrison, Randall P. "Nonverbal Communication: Exploration into Time, Space, Action, and Object." In *Dimensions in Communication*, edited by James H. Campbell and Hal W. Helper. Belmont, CA: Wadsworth, 1965.

Hart, Roderick P. *Modern Rhetorical Criticism.* Glenview, IL: Scott Foresman, 1990.

Horstman, Judith. *The Scientific American Brave New Brain.* San Francisco: Jossey-Bass, 2010.

Hothersall, David. *History of Psychology.* New York: McGraw-Hill, 2004.

Hughes, R. Kent and Bryan Chapell. *1–2 Timothy and Titus.* Wheaton, IL: Crossway, 2000.

Jacks, Robert G. *Getting the Word Across: Speech Communication for Pastors and Lay Leaders.* Grand Rapids: Eerdmans, 1995.

Jamieson, Kathleen Hall. *Eloquence in an Electronic Age: The Transformation of Political Speechmaking.* Oxford: Oxford University Press, 1990.

Kelly, S. D., C. Kravits, and M. Hopking. "Neural Correlates of Bimodal Speech and Gesture Comprehension." *Brain and Language* 89 (2004): 253-60.

Kennedy, George A. *Classical Rhetoric in Its Christian and Secular Tradition from Ancient to Modern Times.* Chapel Hill: University of North Carolina Press, 1980.

Lakoff, George, and Mark Johnson. *Metaphors We Live By.* Chicago: University of Chicago Press, 1980.

Lamb, Lisa Washington. *Blessed and Beautiful: Multiethnic Churches and the Preaching that Sustains Them*. Eugene, OR: Cascade, 2014.

Larsen, David L. *Anatomy of Preaching: Identifying the Issues in Preaching Today*. Grand Rapids: Kregel, 1989.

Lewis, C. S. *Reflections on the Psalms*. London: Geoffrey Bles, 1958.

———. *The Silver Chair*. New York: Macmillan, 1953.

———. *Surprised by Joy: The Shape of My Early Life*. New York: Harcourt, Brace, Jovanovich, 1955.

Llewellyn, Richard. *How Green Was My Valley*. New York: Simon and Schuster, 1939.

Lloyd-Jones, D. Martyn. *Preaching and Preachers*. Grand Rapids: Zondervan, 1971.

Long, Thomas G. *Testimony: Talking Ourselves into Being Christian*. San Francisco: Josey-Bass, 2004.

MacArthur Jr., John. *The MacArthur New Testament Commentary*. Chicago: Moody Press, 1983-2007.

MacDonald, George. *The Gifts of the Christ Child: Fairy Tales and Stories for the Childlike*. Edited by Glenn Edward Sadler. Grand Rapids: Eerdmans, 1973.

Manning, Bernard L. *The Hymns of Wesley and Watts*. Eugene, OR: Wipf and Stock, 1942.

Martin, R. P. *Worship in the Early Church*. Grand Rapids: Eerdmans, 1975.

McAlister, Andrea. "Technology and the Learning Process." *Clavier Companion* (March/April 2015): 20-23.

McDill, Wayne. *The Moment of Truth*. Nashville: B & H, 1999.

McGee, Michael C. "Thematic Reduplication in Christian Rhetoric." *Quarterly Journal of Speech* 56, no. 2 (April 1970): 196-204.

McGrath, Alistair. *C. S. Lewis, A Life: Eccentric Genius, Reluctant Prophet*. Carol Stream, IL: Tyndale, 2014.

McLuhan, Marshall. *The Gutenburg Galaxy*. Toronto: University of Toronto Press, 1962.

Mehrabian, Albert. "Communication Without Words." *Psychology Today* 2 (September 1968): 53.

Micks, Marianne H. *The Future Present: The Phenomenon of Christian Worship*. New York: Seabury, 1970.

Millay, Edna St. Vincent. *Collected Sonnets*. New York: Harper, 1988.

Miller, Steve. *C. H. Spurgeon on Spiritual Leadership.* Chicago: Moody Press, 2003.

Mitchell, Jolyon P. *Visually Speaking: Radio and the Renaissance of Preaching.* Louisville, KY: Westminster John Knox, 1999.

Moore, James. *The Darwin Legend.* Grand Rapids: Baker, 1994.

Novella, Steven. *Your Deceptive Mind: A Scientific Guide to Critical Thinking Skills.* Chantilly, VA: Teaching Company, 2012.

O'Neill, Patrick. "Understanding the Science of the Smile." *The Oregonian,* January 14, 2001: L14.

Overstreet, R. Larry. *Persuasive Preaching: A Biblical and Practical Guide to the Effective Use of Persuasion.* Wooster, OH: Weaver, 2014.

Packer, J. I. *Evangelism and the Sovereignty of God.* Downers Grove, IL: Inter-Varsity Press, 1975.

Parrett, Gary A., and S. Steve Kang. *Teaching the Faith, Forming the Faithful: A Biblical Vision for Education in the Church.* Downers Grove, IL: InterVarsity Press, 2009.

Perelman, Chaim, and L. Olbrechts-Tyteca. *The New Rhetoric: A Treatise on Argumentation.* Notre Dame, IN: University of Notre Dame Press, 1969.

Pfungst, Oskar. *Clever Hans: A Contribution to Experimental Animal and Human Psychology.* Translated by C. L. Rahn. New York: Henry Holt, 1907.

Piper, John. *The Supremacy of God in Preaching.* Rev. ed. Grand Rapids: Baker, 2004.

———. *Desiring God: Meditations of a Christian Hedonist.* Portland, OR: Mult-nomah, 1986.

Pitt-Watson, Ian. *A Primer for Preachers.* Grand Rapids: Baker, 1986.

Plantinga Jr., Corneilius. *Reading for Preaching: The Preacher in Conversation with Storytellers, Biographers, Poets, and Journalists.* Grand Rapids: Eerdmans, 2013.

Plato. *Ion.* Translated by Benjamin Jowett. classics.mit.edu/Plato/ion.html.

———. *Phaedrus.* Translated by W.C. Helmold and W. G. Rabinowitz. Indianapolis: Library of Liberal Arts, 1956.

———. *The Republic.* theoryofmusic.wordpress.com/2008/08/04/music-in-platos-republic.

Postman, Neil. *Amusing Ourselves to Death: Public Discourse in the Age of Show Business.* New York: Penguin, 1985.

Powell, Samuel M. *The Impassioned Life: Reason and Emotion in the Christian Tradition*. Minneapolis: Fortress, 2016.

Price, Charles P. "Remembering and Forgetting in the Old Testament and Its Bearing on the Early Christian Eucharist." ThD diss., Union Theological Seminary, 1962.

Quintilian. *Institutes of Oratory*. Translated by John Selby Watson. London: George Bell & Sons, 1892.

Ralston, Timothy J. "'Remember' and Worship: The Mandate and the Means." *Reformation and Revival* 9, no. 3 (Summer 2000): 77-89.

Ralston, Timothy J. "Scripture in Worship: An Indispensable Symbol of Covenant Renewal." In *Authentic Worship: Hearing Scripture's Voice, Applying Its Truths*, edited by Herbert W. Bateman IV, 195-222. Grand Rapids: Kregel, 2002.

Reed, Eric. "The Preaching Report Card." *Leadership Journal* 20, no. 3 (Summer 1999): www.ctlibrary.com/le/1999/summer/9l3082.html.

Rienstra, Debra, and Ron Rienstra. *Worship Words: Discipling Language for Faithful Ministry*. Grand Rapids: Baker Academic, 2009.

Restak, Richard. *The Naked Brain: How the Emerging Neurosociety is Changing How We Live, Work, and Love*. New York: Three Rivers, 2006.

Sacks, Oliver. *An Anthropologist on Mars: Seven Paradoxical Tales*. New York: Alfred A. Knopf, 1995.

———. *The Man Who Mistook His Wife for a Hat and Other Clinical Tales*. New York: Harper and Row, 1987.

Schaeffer, Francis A. *The God Who Is There*. Vol. 1 of *The Complete Works of Francis A. Schaeffer*. Westchester, IL: Crossway, 1982.

Sitze, Bob. *Your Brain Goes to Church: Neuroscience and Congregational Life*. Herndon, VA: Alban Institute, 2005.

Smith, James K. A. *Imagining the Kingdom: How Worship Works*. Grand Rapids: Baker Academic, 2013.

Spiegel, Alix. "When Memories Never Fade, The Past Can Poison the Present." National Public Radio, December 27, 2013. www.wbur.org/npr/255285479 /when-memories-never-fade-the-past-can-poison-the-present.

Spurgeon, C. H. *Lectures to My Students*. Grand Rapids: Baker, 1978.

Steinbeck, John. *East of Eden*. New York: Penguin, 2002.

Stevenson, Geoffrey. "Learning to Preach: Social Learning Theory and the Development of Christian Preachers." PhD diss., University of Edinburgh, 2009.

Stewart, Charles J., Craig Allen Smith, and Robert E. Denton Jr. *Persuasion in Social Movements*. 2nd ed. Prospect Heights, IL: Waveland, 1989.

Strunk Jr., William, and E. B. White. *The Elements of Style*. 3rd ed. New York: Macmillan, 1979.

Sykes, Marjorie H. "The Eucharist as 'Anamnesis.'" *Expository Times* 71, no. 4 (1960): 115-18.

Thompson, James W. *Preaching Like Paul: Homiletical Wisdom for Today*. Louisville, KY: Westminster John Knox, 2001.

Thonssen, Lester, and A. Craig Baird. *Speech Criticism: The Development of Standards for Rhetorical Appraisal*. New York: Ronald, 1948.

Tolkien, J. R. R. *The Fellowship of the Ring*. New York: Ballantine Books, 1954.

Tracy, J. L., and D. Matsumoto. "The Spontaneous Expression of Pride and Shame: Evidence for Biologically Innate Nonverbal Displays." Proceedings of the National Academy of Sciences 105 (2008): 11655-60.

Van Naaren, R. B., et al. "Mimicry and Prosocial Behavior." *Psychological Science* 15, no. 1 (2009): 71-74.

Volf, Miroslav. *The End of Remembering: Remembering Rightly in a Violent World*. Grand Rapids: Eerdmans, 2006.

Waltke, Bruce. *An Old Testament Theology*. Grand Rapids: Zondervan, 2007.

Weaver, Richard. *The Ethics of Rhetoric*. South Bend, IN: Gateway, 1953.

Whitefield, George. *George Whitefield's Journals*. London: Banner of Truth, 1960.

Wiersbe, Warren W. *Preaching and Teaching With Imagination: The Quest for Biblical Ministry*. Wheaton, IL: Victor, 1994.

Wilson, Paul Scott. *Setting Words on Fire: Putting God at the Center of the Sermon*. Nashville: Abingdon, 2008.

Wood, Julia T. *Interpersonal Communication: Everyday Encounters*. 3rd ed. Belmont, CA: Wadsworth, 2002.

NAME AND SUBJECT INDEX

•

Abraham, x, 16-17, 20, 43, 53, 54, 55, 94

Ambady, Nalini, 111

affections, 4, 57, 59, 65-66, 71, 77

amnesia, 2

analogy. *See* style

Andrewes, Lancelot, 3-5, 8, 23

Apostles, 3, 6, 41, 50, 53-57

Apostles' Creed, 139

Apostrophe. *See* narrative

Aristotle, 62, 69, 88

Augustine, 5, 70, 98, 116

Bacon, Francis, 66

baptism, 68 n5, 136, 142-43

Batten, Patricia, 120

benediction, 139

Blair, Edward, 13, 24, 113

Book of Common Prayer, 21, 143

brain functions
    attention, 4, 13, 28, 33, 36-39, 41, 45, 67-70, 77-79, 81, 87-88, 96, 106, 118-19, 125, 127
    emotion, 3, 14, 16-18, 23, 32, 57 n10, 58-60, 68-69, 72, 75, 79, 87-89, 91, 93, 95, 99, 107-15, 119, 122, 125, 127, 131, 134, 136, 139, 145
    empathy, 45, 91, 113, 118, 120, 123
    engrams, 32, 35-36, 38
    memory, 5 n9, 13 n4, 30-34, 67, 69, 79, 140 n25
    operations of the mind, 67-69
    perception, 32, 33 n12, 34, 37, 57, 113, 119
    schema, 32-34
    smell, 32, 127
    speech, 45, 109
    Zeigarnik effect, 44

brain structures
    axon, 30
    dendrites, 30-32
    hippocampus, 32
    limbic system, 32, 108, 116, 127
    reticular activating system, 33
    synapse, 31
    visual cortex, 32

Brueggemann, Walter, 8, 53

Burke, Kenneth, 88-89

Calvin, John, 39, 130, 133

Campbell, George, 65, 67

Carter, Bryan, 83

ceremony, 3, 5, 50, 64, 125-27, 129, 131-37, 139, 140-43, 145

Clever Hans, 106-7

communion. *See* Lord's Supper

covenant, 4, 6, 8, 16 n5, 17, 19-25, 30, 42, 45, 49-53, 68, 75, 77-78, 84, 90, 92-93, 116, 128-32, 129 n4, 136-7, 140, 143, 147

creeds, 39, 139-42

Dante, 43

Darwin, Charles, 39-40

David, 19, 24, 29, 32, 36, 42, 56, 75-76, 88, 92-95, 116-17, 129, 143

delivery. *See* nonverbal communication

dramatization. *See* narrative

Edwards, Jonathan, 4-5, 59-60, 65, 68-69

emoji, 37

empathy. *See* brain functions

enthymeme. *See* persuasion

eucharist. *See* Lord's Supper

Evans, Tony, 82-83, 100

forgetting
    and accomplishment, 45
    as a blessing, 20, 43
    as a discipline, 8, 43
    and disobedience, 130
    and God, 3, 20, 23-25
    human tendency, 5, 27-29, 31, 63, 68, 110, 126, 136
    and idolatry, 11, 18, 40-41
    as judgment, 18, 24
    and sins, 43-44
    and speaking, 45

Gladwell, Malcolm, 108, 111-12

Guinness, Os, 61

heart. *See* affections

identification. *See* persuasion

imitation, 70-71, 83, 118

incarnation, 19, 95, 105

information overload, 38

indirection/indirect communication, 92-93, 96, 98-99

Keller, Timothy, 99

Lewis, C. S., 11, 27, 41, 47, 69, 90, 94, 98

Lloyd-Jones, Martyn, 119

Lord's Supper, 6, 35, 52, 68 n5, 132-33, 136, 140-42

Luther, Martin, 130, 133

McCheyne, Robert Murray, 117

McLuhan, Marshal, 38

media, 35-39

Mehrabian, Albert, 109

memory
    and belief, 14
    and ceremony, 128-34, 139, 142-45
    and contamination, 34
    as a discipline, 41
    and fading, 3, 15
    and hope, 7, 52
    and humility, 7
    and identity, 8, 53
    and metaphors for it, 5
    and obedience, 7, 29, 56
    and repentance, 7, 44, 78, 92
    with synaesthesia, 30
    and thankfulness, 7
    and warning, 8
    a whole person act, 16-18, 42, 49-50, 58, 68, 91, 108, 114, 127, 132, 139
    and wisdom, 39, 63

and written communication, 38

metaphor. *See* style

Moses, 3, 6, 16, 34, 40-41, 49-53, 55, 57, 79, 92, 129-30, 136

music, 78-80, 88, 118, 120, 129-31, 138, 141

narrative
apostrophe, 98
as a biblical genre, 5, 41
and culture, 5, 87, 88n6, 90, 92
dramatization, 95-98
sermon, 75, 94
testimony, 45, 91-92, 98-100, 143

Nixon-Kennedy debate, 106

nonverbal communication
body language, 107-8, 111-12, 115
extemporaneous speaking, 121
eye contact, 104, 110, 119-22, 124
facial expression, 86, 104, 108-9, 112, 115, 119
first impressions, 111
gestures, 82, 84, 108-9, 119-22, 124, 136
microexpressions, 107
touch (haptics), 110-11
vocal emphasis, 112, 115, 118-24

Novella, Steven, 33-34, 58

offering, 128-29, 132-33, 136, 141

operations of the mind. *See* brain functions

parable, 29, 41, 60, 82, 90, 93, 140

Passover, 6, 35, 50, 127-29, 132-33

Perelman, Chaim, 66-67

persuasion
and apologetics, 61
and collaboration, 55, 63
and emotion/pathos, 59, 96, 114

and enthymeme, 62
and form, 87-89, 88n8, 94
and identification, 91, 93-94, 96, 99
and style, 66, 69, 84
and reason/logos, 59

Piper, John, 73-74

Plato, 38, 80, 113, 130

Polycarp, 101-2

Postman, Neil, 37-38

prayer, 22-23, 45, 55, 99, 116-18, 126, 129-30, 132-33, 143-45, 147

prophets, 36, 41, 50, 52-54, 57

remembrance, 3-6, 8-9, 22-23, 42, 46-52, 56, 58, 63-6, 78, 87, 100, 104, 134, 140, 142-44, 147

repetition, 6, 35, 59, 77-80, 82

rhapsode, 113

rhythm, 78-82, 112, 126, 130

rituals. *See* ceremony

Robinson, Haddon, 75, 96-98, 120

Rogers, Fred, 57-58

sacred space/time, 49-50, 127-28

Sacks, Oliver, 1-2, 47, 85-86, 125

Schaeffer, Francis, 61-62

Scripture reading, 49, 52, 119, 129, 141-42

simile. *See* style

Spurgeon, C. H., 27, 44, 70, 77, 117, 122, 124

story. *See* narrative

style
analogy, 61, 74, 76-77, 94, 100
metaphor, 64, 67, 70, 74-77, 82, 100
oral/written, 35, 38, 78, 104-5, 121, 136
simile, 64, 76

vivacity, 67, 74

symbols. *See* ceremony

testimony. *See* narrative

Twain, Mark, 96, 137-38

vivacity. *See* style

Waltke, Bruce, 13

Weaver, Richard, 66, 70

Wesley, Charles, 25

Wesley, John, 130

worship, 4, 8, 16, 18, 21, 29, 40, 48-9, 58, 77, 95, 117-8, 120, 128-36, 133n14, 134 n18, 138-39, 143-45, 147

SCRIPTURE INDEX

•

OLD TESTAMENT

Genesis
6:5, *57*
8:1, *19*
9:13, *3*
9:15, *19*
12:2, *20*
19:26, *43*
19:29, *19*
30:22, *19*
40, *16*
40:23, *16*
41:9, *16*

Exodus
2:24, *17*
12:26, *128*
17:14, *24*
20:8, *16, 127*
23:14, *127*
28:12, *129*
28:29, *129*

Leviticus
2:2, *129*
5:12, *129*

6:15, *129*
16:1, *128*
24:7, *129*
26:42, *20*

Numbers
5:26, *129*
6:24-26, *139*
10:9, *19*
15:37, *128*
21, *136*
21:6, *34*
29:7, *128*

Deuteronomy
1:27, *42*
1:30, *42*
4:9, *42, 50*
4:39, *50*
5:15, *50*
6:4, *40, 79*
6:9, *128*
6:12, *50*
6:20, *51*
7:18, *50*
8:2, *50*
8:11, *18, 41*

8:14, *50*
8:19, *18*
9:7, *92*
11, *137*
11:18, *50, 128*
15:15, *16, 92*
16:12, *50*
16:17, *136*
17:14, *128*
17:18, *28, 137*
24:17, *8*
24:22, *50*
25:17, *50*
26:5, *7*
26:6, *51*
26:13, *50*
28:47, *57*
28:49, *52*
29:15, *51*
31:9, *51*
31:19, *129*
32:7, *50*
32:26, *24*

Joshua
1:13, *16*
1:16, *16*

4:1, *126*
7:25, *126*
8:29, *126*
8:30, *126, 129, 136*

Judges
3:7, *18*
8:34, *29*
16:28, *22*

Ruth
1:16-17, *80*

1 Samuel
1:8, *57*
17:34, *42*
30:6, *117*

2 Samuel
8:15, *4*
12:1-15, *92*
12:7, *29*
18:18, *24*

1 Kings
4:3, *4*

2 Kings
6:11, *57*
18, *136*
18:4, *34*
18:18, *4*
18:37, *4*
23:2, *129*

1 Chronicles
16:4, *129*
18:15, *4*
29:10, *143*

2 Chronicles
34:8, *4*

Nehemiah
5:19, *24*
13:14, *24*
13:22, *24*
13:31, *24*

Esther
9:26, *136*
9:28, *17*

Job
7:7, *22*
18:17, *24*

Psalms
3:3, *144*
5:2, *144*
7:9, *144*
7:17, *144*
8:4, *18*
9:5, *24*
18:2, *144*
47, *51*
54:4, *144*
56, *19*
56:1, *19*
56:5, *19*
56:6, *19*
56:8, *19*
59:5, *145*
65:5, *145*
71:5, *145*
71:22, *145*
73, *120, 122*
74:22, *22*
77, *45*

77:7, *7*
77:11, *7, 45, 46*
77:13, *46*
78, *50*
78:39, *18*
89, *22*
89:50, *22*
90, *139*
90:5, *18*
94:1, *145*
94:2, *145*
95:2, *138*
99:4, *145*
103:14, *18*
103:17, *17*
105:1, *7*
105:5, *7*
106:21, *29*
114:3, *51*
115:12, *19*
119:16, *18*
119:109, *18*
124:8, *138*
125:2, *128*
136:23, *19*
136:26, *145*
137, *127*
137:4, *127*
145:18, *138*

Proverbs
3, *21*
3:9, *137*
4:23, *57*
10:7, *24*
16:1, *57*
16:9, *57*
23:7, *57*

Ecclesiastes
9:5, *24*

Isaiah
1:18, *24*
26:14, *24*
28, *78*
28:10, *79*
36:3, *4*
36:22, *4*
49:14, *18*
49:15, *11*
49:16, *25*
51:1, *52*
53, *141*
54:9, *53*
55:6, *138*
56:5, *24*
57:8, *40*
57:11, *40*
62:6-7, *129*

Jeremiah
7:9, *52*
11:19, *24*
51:50, *8*

Lamentations
5:1, *22*

Ezekiel
16, *74, 77*

Hosea
4:6, *18*

Amos
2:10, *52*

Habakkuk
1:5, *52*
3:17, *131*

NEW TESTAMENT
Matthew
6:24, *40*
6:25, *116*
7:24, *82*
13:34, *85*
16:9, *29*
18:20, *135*
18:23, *29*
24:27, *73*
25, *96*
26:26, *133*
26:75, *7*
28:20, *60, 135*

Mark
4:1, *41*
4:19, *41*
9:16, *58*
14:9, *8*
14:22, *133*

Luke
1:72, *20*
9:62, *43*
10:25, *76*
17:32, *4, 8*
22:14, *133*
22:16, *140*
22:18, *140*
22:60, *110*
23:42, *11, 13*
24:27, *64*

John
2:22, *29*
5:35, *59*
12:16, *29*
14:1, *57*
14:18, *17*
14:26, *9, 17, 64*
16:4, *29*

Acts
2:37, *58*
2:42, *133*
2:46, *133*
8:22, *57*
10:4, *129*
13:2, *132*

Romans
1:1, *56*
1:18, *21*
1:28, *21*
2:1, *21*
6:3, *54*
6:16, *54*
8, *80*
8:35, *80*
11:2, *54*
15:14, *54*
15:33, *139*

1 Corinthians
2:11, *64*
3:16, *54*
5:4, *135*
5:6, *54*
6:19, *132*
10, *91*
10:1, *42*
10:11, *91*

10:16, *140*
11, *141*
11:17, *133, 142*
11:23, *133*
11:26, *140, 142*
13:7, *80*
14:23, *135*
14:25, *134*
15:1, *56*
15:20, *56*

2 Corinthians
5:11, *61*
8:8, *56*

Galatians
1:14, *45*
2:10, *16*

Ephesians
1:6, *71*
2:11, *54*
2:13, *45*
2:21, *132*
4:1, *141*

Philippians
3:1, *54*
3:5, *45*

Colossians
1:28, *60*
3:5, *40*
3:16, *129, 133*
3:17, *139*
4:18, *16*

1 Thessalonians
4:13, *56*
5:11, *138*

1 Timothy
2:7, *60*
4:13, *129, 137*

2 Timothy
1:3, *55*
1:4, *55*
1:6, *55*
1:11, *60*
1:13, *55*
2:8, *25, 56, 116, 130*
2:14, *56*
3:14, *55*

Hebrews
1, *76*
1:2, *76*
2:1, 4, *39*
4:15, *19*
8:5, *132*
10:1, *131*
10:11, *20*
11, *54*
11:13, *43*
12:5-6, *21*
12:18, *42*
12:22, *135*
13:3, *17*
13:5, *20*
13:7, *17*
13:15, *132*
13:16, *137*

James
1:22, *28*
2:20, *55*
4:14, *18*

1 Peter
1:3, *116*

2 Peter
1:9, *63*
1:12, *6*
1:13, *54*
3:1, *54*

1 John
2:7, *54*
3:16, *56*
5:21, *41*

Jude
3, *9*
5, *54*
17, *54*
20–21, *116*
21, *41, 116*

Revelation
2:4, *63*
2:5, *17*
2:8, *101*
2:10, *101*
3:1, *63*
3:3, *17*
12:10, *44*
16:19, *21*
18:5, *21*
19, *116*

Finding the Textbook You Need

The IVP Academic Textbook Selector
is an online tool for instantly finding the IVP books
suitable for over 250 courses across 24 disciplines.

-----

ivpacademic.com